# REVIEWS FOR

## *Transformed by The Spirit*

Craig Prather's gentle and inviting book punctuated with basic spiritual formation principles appropriately interlaced with his own personal transformational journey serves to encourage Christ-followers to engage in the process of spiritual transformation.

—**Calvin Blom, D.Min.**, *Spiritual Director*

✶✶✶

Craig Prather combines historic Christian tradition with his lived experience to produce this introspective and deep resource on spiritual formation. Transformed by the Spirit is a helpful guide for anyone who is eager to grow in Christlikeness.

—**Brandon Evans, Pastor**, *D.Min. (ABD)*

✶✶✶

Transformed by the Spirit is a well thought out piece looking into the historical ideal of Spiritual Formation. Pr. Craig gives us some amazing ideas into how we can develop a closer relationship with

Jesus Christ. This is a book that will be read several times to grasp all the ideas offered.

—**Rev. Michael Patterson**, *Episcopal Priest*

***

In Transformed by the Spirit, Craig Prather takes our hands and our hearts and leads us on a spiritual journey filled with historical examples of fellow travelers, rules for the road, obstacles to avoid, and travel tips to stay connected to the One who knows exactly what speed we need to go in our journey of becoming like Jesus. Instead of arriving at our destination tired, weary and exhausted, we will lock arms with others and rejoice that we, by the Spirit, have finished the journey well.

—**Dr. Tom Schiave**, *Lead Pastor at Gateway Church and Professor in the Pastoral Ministries Dept. at Multnomah Biblical Seminary.*

***

Craig's work is a gift to society during a time when fear, anger, and violence are leaving many with distance and absence as far too prominent metaphors for trying to stand on much greater spiritual horizons, such as faith, hope, and love. Reaching back to retrieve from trusted voices in the Scriptures and long traditions, to contemporary guides, such as Dallas Willard, Craig's book will open many thresholds for understanding how being formed in Christ through the Spirit transforms everything.

—**T.M. Allen (PhD**), *Pastor at New Life Church*

Transformed by the Spirit

A Modern Journey into Spiritual
Formation

CRAIG M. PRATHER

Published by KHARIS PUBLISHING, imprint of KHARIS MEDIA LLC.

Copyright © 2020 Craig M. Prather

ISBN-13:978-1-946277-81-7
ISBN-10: 1-946277-81-9

Library of Congress Control Number: 2020921184

All KHARIS PUBLISHING products are available at special quantity discounts for bulk purchase for sales promotions, premiums, fund-raising, and educational needs. For details, contact:

Kharis Media LLC
Tel: 1-479-599-8657
support@kharispublishing.com
www.kharispublishing.com

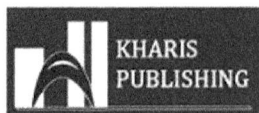

To my loving and brilliant professors, Dr. Thomas Schiave and Dr. Calvin Blom. Thank you both for your kindness and patience with me during my academic journey into spiritual formation.

# CONTENTS

# FOREWORD

Tony Slavin, a most beloved colleague, has oriented his life and his ministerial word around the Apostle Paul's words in Galatians 4:19, "Until Christ is formed in you."

Paul also describes his passion for this by preceding this phrase with a metaphor of a woman going through labor pains. This is not a casual comment for Paul. This reflects Paul's motivation for what he writes and what he does. It is a mission deeply embedded in his soul. In doing so, Paul displays his singular passion and the frenetic intensity he feels about this effort.

Tony shares this passion, as do I. As a minister, I have preached many sermons. I have counseled many people, and I have listened intently to the story of people's lives and have worked hard for the Kingdom of God. After all of these years, I have come to the conclusion that Christ-Formation (*or Spiritual Transformation*) is the most important goal of life.

Tragically, this does not seem to be the reason that most people go to church, or involve themselves in communities of faith. Most people simply want to be better versions of themselves; or to meet some other emotional need, like fellowship. They stay busy in the faith, they do things as substitutes for doing other detrimental activities that might be self-harming. Rarely do most people think about the state of their soul.

For the Apostle Paul, Spiritual Formation is an important measurement for all believers. These words also reflect that upon salvation, we are not finished works. This can be confusing because the scriptures imply perfection on account of Jesus' work and His own words on the cross, "It is finished." These words may speak to atonement, satisfying God's wrath and eternal punishment. They may also speak to justification in the same way that Martin Luther and the Apostle Paul believed that we are saved by faith and not works (Rom. 1:17, Eph. 2:8). However, it does not speak to the state of the soul. Deep down we know that we are still works in progress.

There exists a gap between how we are and what we should be, or what we can be; Christ is not fully formed in us.

The question then is how does Spiritual Formation occur? I believe that it is not something that happens without effort. By this, I don't mean work—I mean effort; intentional introspection, spiritual devotion, and an intimate relationship with God. It is also the direct result and the focus of the Holy Spirit's work.

This author, Professor/Pastor Craig Prather, is also committed toward this same passion. The passion of Paul, the passion of Tony, and my own passion, is to see people grow in the faith, to grow in Christ's image, and to grow in awareness of their own identity as desired by God.

Readers should expect Professor Prather to easily lay out the rationale for spiritual growth. His work in this book is important. Craig lays out an argument for this work. He presents a brief history of Spiritual Formation and anchors it to three important principles: Christ's likeness, personal relationship with God, and the discovery of our personal identity.

It is my hope that readers will narrow their vision for spiritual growth with laser-like targeting. I also hope that they will deepen in their relationship with God's precious Holy Spirit. And even more, I hope that they will have an epiphany of who they really are in terms of personal identity. I remember a story that I once read—two angels rising into the heavenly atmosphere were speaking about the state of man. One angel said to the other, "Do you think that we should tell them (*man*) what they really are?" The other angel replied, "If we did, they'd never believe it."

~ *Sincerely,*

**John McKendricks** *D.Min (ABD)., M.Div.*

# ACKNOWLEDGMENTS

I'd like to thank my dear friends and family, instructors, and colleagues for their inspiration, patience, kindness, and guidance in my spiritual, academic, and professional life. Including, but certainly not limited to:

*My beautiful Lord and Savior, Jesus Christ, My beautiful wife and children.* Dr. Tom Schiave, Dr. Calvin Blom, Dr. Cesar Minera, Dr. John McKendricks, Dr. Doug Vaughan, Dr. Timothy Allen, Dr. Paul Louis Metzger, Dr. Barbara Feil, Dr. Donny Crandell, Professor Mike Preston, Professor Tony Slavin, Professor Kristopher Dahir, Professor Jay Hull, Professor Allen Battle, Rev. Mike Patterson, Rev. Jonathan Oetting, Paul Gulck, and David Quinn.

# List of Abbreviations

## Old Testament

| | |
|---|---|
| Gen. | Genesis |
| Exod. | Exodus |
| Lev. | Leviticus |
| Num. | Numbers |
| Deut. | Deuteronomy |
| Josh. | Joshua |
| Judg. | Judges |
| Ruth | Ruth |
| 1-2 Sam. | 1-2 Samuel |
| 1-2 Kgs. | 1-2 Kings |
| 1-2 Chr. | 1-2 Chronicles |
| Ezra | Ezra |
| Neh. | Nehemiah |
| Esth. | Esther |
| Job | Job |
| Ps/Pss. | Psalm/Psalms |
| Prov. | Proverbs |
| Eccl. (Qoh) | Ecclesiastes (Qoheleth) |
| Song. (Cant) | Song of Songs/Solomon (Canticles) |

Transformed by The Spirit

| Isa. | Isaiah |
| Jer. | Jeremiah |
| Lam. | Lamentations |
| Ezek. | Ezekiel |
| Dan. | Daniel |
| Hos. | Hosea |
| Joel | Joel |
| Amos | Amos |
| Obad. | Obadiah |
| Jonah | Jonah |
| Mic. | Micah |
| Nah. | Nahum |
| Hab. | Habakkuk |
| Zeph. | Zephaniah |
| Hag. | Haggai |
| Zech. | Zechariah |
| Mal. | Malachi |

## New Testament

| | |
|---|---|
| Matt. | Matthew |
| Mark | Mark |
| Luke | Luke |
| John | John |
| Acts | Acts |
| Rom. | Romans |
| 1-2 Cor. | Corinthians |
| Gal. | Galatians |
| Eph. | Ephesians |
| Phil. | Philippians |
| Col. | Colossians |
| 1-2 Thess. | 1-2 Thessalonians |
| 1-2 Tim. | 1-2 Timothy |
| Titus | Titus |
| Phlm. | Philemon |
| Heb. | Hebrews |
| Jas. | James |
| 1-2 Pet. | 1-2 Peter |
| 1-2-3 John | 1-2-3 John |
| Jude | Jude |
| Rev. | Revelation |

# INTRODUCTION

In the late spring of 1986, I was invited to a small Lutheran Church by my childhood friend, Paul. I enjoyed the service so much that I asked to go again the following week. This pattern of attending church, then afterward eating a great brunch consisting of eggs, waffles, and French toast that Paul's mother would cook for us continued for the next six years. Around the age of sixteen, I took a break from church for a while and spent some time getting to know myself. It's funny how independent one becomes once they get their driver's license.

The Lutheran Church (at that time) didn't have any resources or "how-to" guides on spiritual formation and growth, apart from the Bible. It wasn't until after many heartbreaks, poor decisions, relationship failures, and depression that I began to seek God again and work on bettering my relationship with Him. In my early twenties—after my divorce with my oldest son's mom—I decided to join a small, non-denominational church in Sparks, Nevada. As I sat in the back row of the hundred-something member congregation, I tried to drink in the weekly messages and motivational metaphors that the pastor shared with us. Week after week, I would force myself to wake up and drive to the service, feeling as though God was pulling me there. Many family members suggested that I seek medical help for my bouts with depression instead.

I did eventually see a psychologist, who recommended medication for depression. But after taking the jagged little pills, which made me feel out of it and dizzy most of the time, I prayed that God would intervene. As I drove east towards Las Vegas with a full bottle of Aspirin in my hand, I pulled over and started to open the lid. Just then, a voice inside me said, *Turn around.* I drove two hundred miles back to my parents' house where I cried uncontrollably, both in shame and in joy that the God of the entire universe would take the time to help a poor sinner like me.

God often steps into our lives when we least expect it. In my case,

God's timing couldn't have been better. I was a confused, depressed, and insecure twenty-something who had just gone through a divorce with a small child involved and didn't have the least idea how to handle it. Perhaps, you can relate to my story? Perhaps, you have had times in your life when you question whether or not God is really there? Does He care about what you're going through, what you've already been through, or what you've suffered? From my own personal experience, I can assure you that the answer to these questions is always yes. Sometimes we are too blinded by our sins to see His loving face shining before us.

In my first book, *Moved by the Spirit,* my goal was to invite the reader to go on a journey with me as I highlighted some of the experiences that I'd had with God as I pursued Him more aggressively. My intention was—and always will be—to give glory to God through my writing and theological insights. My subsequent goal is to share with the audience ways in which we can relate to our creator in more meaningful and productive ways, and that is the principal goal of this book. I've included several book reviews, outlines, and other resources that I put together in Seminary that are sprinkled throughout the text, as well as in the appendix section. My hope is that you can use this text for academic study, in your small groups or young adult ministry classes, or when teaching on spiritual formation in general.

Over the past seven and a half years of taking both undergraduate and graduate courses at Multnomah University & Seminary School, I've developed a passion for spiritual formation. Many thanks to Dr. Calvin Blom for his patience, guidance, assistance in the revision process, source materials, and literary contributions to this volume. This book would not be the studious text presented before you without his support.

Dallas Willard once said, "Spiritual progressions always conclude with *agape,* or 'divine love' at the center."[1] Indeed, love should be at the center of all things if we are to have hearts after God's own heart. You may recall

---

[1] Willard, "Spiritual Formation: What it is, and How it is done," accessed January 7, 2020, http://www.dwillard.org/articles/individual/spiritual-formation-what-it-is-and-how-it-is-done.

reading about the famous David and Bathsheba story in 2 Samuel, and how David sinned greatly against both God and his mistress. But, do you remember what God told King Saul when David was still quite young? He said, *"Now your kingdom shall not continue. The Lord has sought out a man after his own heart, and the Lord has commanded him to be prince over his people because you have not kept what the Lord commanded you."*[2]

God always judges us by our hearts, which is why love can cover a multitude of sins. The flesh is something, I'm afraid, we cannot live without while we continue to inhabit this earth. Yet God works with us in our sinful nature and helps us to counter our evil thoughts and desires through the power of His Holy Spirit. When God looks at born-again Christians, He does not see the outward appearance. Rather, He sees the finished product. God, who was once *with* us in the form of Christ Jesus, now dwells *in* us in the form of the Holy Spirit (see Romans 8:9-10).

I pray that this book will be both informational and spiritually edifying to your soul. This text is not intended to be a comprehensive guide to all things related to spiritual formation. Instead, it is meant to be one of many tools in your spiritual tool belt that you can re-read or reference as needed. Many, many hours of research and time with the Father have gone into putting this text together; I truly cherish the opportunity to share these godly insights with you.

# Pax Vobis,

Craig M. Prather

---

[2] 1 Sam. 13:14 (English Standard Version).

# CHAPTER 1

## Relational Theology

Many churchgoers invest minimal time in their relationships with Jesus Christ but knowing Christ is part of eternal life.[3] Not just knowing Christ by name, but knowing Him on an intimate level. The Apostle Peter tells us that we must grow in grace and knowledge.[4] The Greek word that Peter uses for knowledge is γνῶσις, which infers a sense of divine and intimate knowledge of someone or something.[5] I've met a lot of people over the years, in a variety of churches who all claim to be devout Christians. They joyfully sing along with the worship songs, clap their hands and shout "Amen!" at the clever quips of the pastor. They regularly attend the Sunday morning church services week after week; some spending decades in the pews of the parish or serving on a variety of church councils. Yet, many of them cannot quote any favorite passages from the Bible or tell me when they previously spent time alone with God, or even reflect on when they last prayed in silence for someone that they did not personally know. God knows every single hair on our heads (see Luke 12:7); Christianity must be a two-way relationship.

I can't be too hard on these people because many years ago, I was one of them. I started attending church at a relatively young age. I was the only Christian in the family. My parents never discouraged my church involvement, but being atheists, they never participated in it either. I stumbled up-

---

[3] See John 17:3.
[4] See 2 Pet. 3:18.
[5] See BDAG, *A Greek-English Lexicon of the New Testament and Other Early Christian Literature*, 203.

on a small ELCA Lutheran church in 1986 via the invite of my best friend, Paul. Quite often, God likes to use others as instruments to carry out His divine will. One might even say, God chose *me* before the foundation of the world.[6] Though I began my journey with Christ at a young age, I hadn't approached the place of confidence in my relationship with Him that I am at today without many trials and setbacks.

Obedience wasn't always my strong suit. Perhaps, it stems from the many rebellious years during my adolescence, in which I acted malevolently against the desperate biddings of my parents. Or maybe I simply felt that I knew what was best for my life, no matter what other, wiser confidants suggested. Regardless of my personal justification in these situations, I always have Jesus Christ in my corner, helping me through hardships, crying with me during trials, building me up when I feel down, and accepting my forgiveness when I ask for it. He has never abandoned me, nor forsaken me.

It seems quite apparent that though people are content with believing in Jesus Christ and the salvific work that He accomplished for us on the cross, there are few intentions of growing in faith or in a relationship with Him. This is where spiritual formation comes in.

According to Dallas Willard:

> *Spiritual formation in the tradition of Jesus Christ is the process of transformation of the inmost dimension of the human being, the heart, which is the same as the spirit or will. It is being formed (really, transformed) in such a way that its natural expression comes to be the deeds of Christ done in the power of Christ.*[7]

In other words, spiritual formation involves transforming into Christ-likeness through the power of the Holy Spirit using spiritual disciplines. The Apostle John tells us that without Jesus we can do nothing.[8] So, along with

---

[6] Eph. 1:4 (Emphasis mine).
[7] Willard, "Spiritual Formation: What it is, and How it is done," accessed April 17, 2020, http://www.dwillard.org/articles/individual/spiritual-formation-what-it-is-and-how-it-is-done.
[8] John 15:5 (Emphasis mine).

the help of the Holy Spirit, we actively participate in this transformation process. Yet, spiritual formation does not solely take place via the spiritual disciplines. God uses our everyday life experiences, whether we like them or not, to grow us in Him. Reliance on the Holy Spirit and the disciplines are volitional actions that we can proactively take, but God can—and does—use other means as well. However, not all faith traditions agree that *we* need to be entwined in this process.

The human yearning for something more is the desire for spiritual formation. From the earliest disciples—faithful Jewish men and women—who saw something more in Jesus' life, to present-day persons, spiritual formation is the desire for a deeper more authentic life in Christ.

Very few churches have spiritual formation ministries, especially smaller churches, which is why the need for spiritual formation ministries exists. Spiritual formation is not a new concept. In fact, people like Kenneth Boa, Dallas Willard, Rick Warren, Bill Thrall, Jack Hayford, the Reformers to the medieval theologians, the desert fathers to the disciples themselves, were all working on spiritual formation and spiritual growth in one way or another.

Spiritual formation is important because God designed us to be in relationship with Him, as well as with each other. My Greek professor, of all people, told me once that pastoral care is where you will spend the majority of your time in ministry. This is so true. I hardly ever receive theological questions from my congregation; however, I regularly encounter several questions about how to deal with a certain situation or struggle. This is why it's imperative to have tools in our spiritual tool belts that help guide and direct others towards Christlikeness.

Not long ago, I had attended a Sunday morning service at a local conservative Lutheran church and brought up this need to the pastor. Quite uncouthly, he responded that my views on trying to hinder sinful thoughts and actions were "works based statements," and nothing that Jesus or the gospel stood for. I must admit, this response had my stomach in all kinds of knots. Was I wrong in my quest to be more Christlike? Should I simply ask forgiveness every time I sin, then go to bed at night sleeping soundly; knowing that my salvation is secure in Christ regardless of my disobedience? Shouldn't it bother God that I continue to sin because I'm not actively pursuing a closer relationship with Him; utilizing spiritual disciplines to fight against the powers of the world, the flesh, and the devil? Does the Lutheran dichotomy of Law & Gospel combine, rather than separate "mirror and guide" as pertaining to the three purposes of the Law? Was this indeed a grave misrepresentation of Luther's doctrines of Sola Gratia and Sola Fide? After all, the author of Hebrews did say, *"If we deliberately keep on sinning after we have received the knowledge of the truth, no sacrifice for sins is left, but only a fearful expectation of judgment and of raging fire that will consume the enemies of God."* [9]

Changing our behaviors can only happen if we are willing to make the change. As it would turn out, Dr. Tom Schiave, one of my beloved spiritual formation professors, had me read a book by Kent Carlson and Mike Lueken titled, *Renovation of the Church.* In one of the latter chapters, Lueken states that change can only occur if our intention is to allow the Holy Spirit to change us. He further remarks:

We talk about the various spiritual disciplines we can practice creating space for God in our hearts. But we don't talk as much about our will or our intention. The Holy Spirit will never usurp our will. If we don't want Christ formed in us, then not even the Spirit will make it happen. [10]

And perhaps, that is the true problem. I thought about Lueken's words for quite some time. They pierced me to the heart and opened my mind to the possibility that it might be me who was hindering the Holy Spirit's work in my life. Could it be, that despite my best efforts, the Spirit was being held captive by my own fleshly desires? Growing into Christlikeness is an unpretentious paradox. We cannot get there through complete passivity; we cannot progress in our walk through our own fleshly efforts. We can only get to a place of perfection in Christ by our willingness to participate with the Holy Spirit in allowing our hearts to be changed from a heart of stone to a heart of flesh.

No sin is too small for God to simply ignore. When I wrote my first published devotional, *Moved by the Spirit,* I allowed the Spirit to wash over me while I was writing. Not only were my thoughts presented to the audience, but also the thoughts of the Holy Spirit, Himself, which are pure and devoid of sinful influence. One of the texts that inspired me to write such a devotional was *God Seekers* by Richard H. Schmidt. *God Seekers* is a collection of extant Christian spiritualities, written by some of the most well-

---

[9] Heb. 10:26-27 (New International Version).
[10] Carlson & Lueken, *Renovation of the Church,* 121.

known theologians of the past twenty centuries. Medieval theologian, Anselm, once wrote:

Maybe you think a particular sin is small. Would that the strict judge would regard any sin as small! But, poor me, any and every sin dishonors God because it disobeys his laws. So where is the sinner who presumes to call some sin small? How small a thing is it to dishonor God?[11]

Any sin that is committed is indeed dishonoring to the Father, yet sometimes we cannot prevent ourselves from sinning—at least not in our minds. This is an unfortunate paradox that we, as human beings, often find ourselves in. Perhaps, a relatable Scripture can be found in 1 Kings when King Solomon blesses the temple that contained the Ark of the Covenant:

When they sin against you—<u>for there is no one who does not sin</u>—and you become angry with them and give them over to their enemies, who take them captive to their own lands, far away or near; and if they have a change of heart in the land where they are held captive, and repent and plead with you in the land of their captors and say, 'We have sinned, we have done wrong, we have acted wickedly'; and if they turn back to you with all their heart and soul in the land of their enemies who took them captive, and pray to you toward the land you gave their ancestors, toward the city you have chosen and the temple I have built for your Name; then from heaven, your dwelling place, hear their prayer and their plea, and uphold their cause. And forgive your people, who have sinned against you; forgive all the offenses they have committed against you and cause their captors to show them mercy.[12]

Achieving a sinless state of being is not realistic during our time on this earth. The Apostle John echoes the revelation that we are not, and perhaps cannot be, fully "sin-free;" at least not in this lifetime.[13] Yet, that does not mean that we throw in the towel and give in to every fleshly desire. What matters to God is not that we sometimes fail in our efforts; what matters to God is that we don't give up in trying to become better representations of Him. If it had distressed God so much that we could not achieve a sinless state on our own, then surely, He would have not put a plan into

---

[11] Anselm, *Meditation on Fear*, 100.
[12] 1 Kgs 8:46-50 (NIV).
[13] See John 1:8.

motion to save us from the eternal consequences of our sins. We must always try to saunter in obedience, but when we slip and fall, realize that Jesus Christ is constantly there to pick us back up.

Another section in *Renovation of the Church* spoke directly to some of the issues mentioned earlier, as I attempted to re-familiarize myself with the Lutheran Church tradition. Sadly, when I proposed starting up a workshop in spiritual formation for the congregants, I received little to no encouraging response. Looking more into Lutheran theology, it appeared that some consider sanctification a finished process following our justification. So, in certain Lutherans' minds, we need not work on ourselves, we simply must enjoy God's grace and ask forgiveness of our sins.[14] Yet, sanctification should be viewed differently. Having been "fully sanctified," as it pertains to our current earthly existence, simply doesn't align with how we treat each other outwardly or how we secretly indulge in our sins inwardly. Our sanctification is progressive and requires our intentional participation (see 2 Cor. 3:18). In addition, Lueken adds:

> *Our passivity in our spiritual growth is a hangover from the Reformation. We are afraid of turning grace into works. So instead, we turn grace into a divine magic that does everything for us. But to experience spiritual formation in Christ, we have to want Christ formed in us. This has nothing to do with earning God's favor; it has to do with how we respond to the undeserved grace of God.[15]*

*Godly Relationships*

Strong godly relationships are essential in our spiritual growth. Not long after my baptism, did I venture out in search of other like-minded Christians. Expecting to find holiness in adolescence is like running uphill backwards with bare feet. In other words, I found that sin in my life seemed to only increase. The more I tried to run from it, the more I would slip and fall. Instead of repelling sin from my thoughts and desires, I seemed to welcome it with open arms. Sure, I believed in Jesus Christ, studied about Him,

---

[14] In fairness to other Lutheran Church denominations, the concept of finished sanctification is not a complete consensus, even among the more conservative branches. See, Dr. Jordan Cooper, "Progressive Sanctification: A Lutheran Doctrine," JustandSinner.com, April 7, 2013, http://www.justandsinner.com.

[15] Carlson & Lueken, *Renovation of the Church*, 122.

prayed, worshiped, and felt love for Him, but I wasn't living like it. For me, Christianity wasn't a light switch that I could flip on and suddenly all of my temptations would disappear, it was more like a dimmer switch that sometimes shone brightly, and other times I could barely navigate my way through a dimly lit corridor. I enjoyed my new life in Christ, but I still wanted to hang on to my old life as well. This is why stronger godly relationships matter. Author and theologian, Stanley Grenz, notes:

> *There is a great difference between knowing God and possessing propositional knowledge about God. When we know God, we have more than merely a body of truths about God. More importantly, we know the living and personal God. The task of knowing God, then, does not focus on the possession of a list of statements about God, but on the enjoyment of fellowship with God.*[16]

God is very personal. One of my favorite stories of the Old Testament can be found in Genesis, chapter two. What I love about the creation narrative is that God's greatest masterpiece…is us. Forming Adam from the ground as a potter forms his clay, God demonstrates how intimately relational He truly is. This relationship is multifaceted; starting within Himself, spreading to creation, and finally culminating with us. The Lord God is not someone who speaks creation into existence and then steps away to watch it unfold, like a watchmaker who winds up a clock only to allow it to unravel, untouched, before his very eyes. No, my friends, our God is intimately active in our lives at every moment; interacting with us, guiding us, believing in us. If we would only take the time to listen to Him, we would live much healthier lives. He has always been in relationship with us, and He will always *be* in relationship with us.

Both rest and reflection are essential components of building our relationship with God. God had just finished six days' worth of creation and then He rested. God's rest was not due to the fact that he was physically exhausted from the laborious task of speaking creation into being, but rather, God rested to set a future example of its importance for all of mankind; culminating in our final rest in Jesus Christ. New Testament Professor, Karen H. Jobes, explains that God's rest is not putting His feet up and relaxing after the exertion of creating the universe; rather, the cosmological context of Genesis 2:2 refers to a deity resting, or *sitting* in a temple—and

---

[16] Grenz, *Theology for the Community of God*, 49.

*only* in a temple. This took place as a result of a crisis being resolved or when stability had been achieved.[17] We now have rest in Jesus Christ because of our redemption from sin. The Book of Exodus tells us, "You must observe my Sabbaths. This will be a sign between me and you *for the generations to come*, so you know that I am the Lord who makes you holy."[18] We are commanded to rest in Him because when God rested from His work, He took up His rightful place as ruler of the universe that He had created. The Sabbath is for recognizing that it is God who provides for us and who is the master of our lives and our world.[19]

Much like we need to reflect on our creator during relaxation, we also need to reflect upon God regarding our, sometimes unstable, earthly relationships. Human beings are inherently relational. Healthy relationships with God and with each other help to create unity within the body of Christ. Francis Frangipane once said:

Oneness is at the core of the divine nature. If we will be brought into the divine likeness, our goal must also be to walk in oneness with God; and through Him, oneness with other Christians. If we will grow, we will see that the natural outcome of the workings of God will unfold into perfecting God's people into a unit.[20]

As mentioned, God is relational within Himself. The doctrine of the Trinity demonstrates that the Father, Son, and Holy Spirit all exist in perfect harmony and unity as one. The word trinity means, "tri-unity" or "three-in-oneness." The Triune God enters into a relationship with the world He creates.[21] God made mankind in His image to both glorify Himself and to have a relationship with us.

We were never meant to live alone. Verse seven, of Genesis chapter two, tells us that God formed man from the ground. The Hebrew word for ground used here is, *Adamah*. Thus, Adam was formed. The word for Spirit of God, or breath of God, in Hebrew is the word *Ruach Elohim*.[22] Indeed, it

---

[17] Jobes, *Letters to the Church*, 129.
[18] Ex. 31:13 (Emphasis mine).
[19] Jobes, *Letters to the Church*, 130.
[20] Frangipane, *Unity*, 7.
[21] Grudem, *Systematic Theology*, 227.
[22] Parsons, "Hebrew Names of God," Hebrew4Christians.com, accessed October 20, 2017,

was the very breath of God that was used to bring Adam to life. It is this same breath of God that gives us new life through the power of the Holy Spirit at conversion. After the creation of Adam, we see the first place in the narrative where God says, "It is not good." Indicating, it was not good for man to be alone. At the conclusion of each day, God says, "It was good." The exception shows God's concern that Adam has a partner like his own kind; demonstrating again the relational aspect of creation. Dr. Terence E Fretheim notes that:

> *God has identified a problem within the divine creative work and moves to find a solution, to make those changes that would enable a different evaluation: it is now good. Notably, relationship with at least one other human being is considered essential for human beings to be evaluated as "good."*[23]

Studies have shown that people are generally happier when they are in healthy relationships. Don't be fooled by the postings on social media that proclaim how prodigious things are if we remain single. Eve was created from Adam, but not created to serve Adam. The order of creation is spiritual in headship, and not necessarily a female to male subordination. Adam and Eve were both tasked with taking care of the garden together. The Fall had disrupted the harmony that originally existed in God's creation. As a correction of that disruption, the two that become one flesh once again complement each other, and also unify as one in Christ. Theologian, Matthew Henry, explains this dichotomy of subordination and union quite well:

> *Adam was first formed, then Eve, and she was made of the man, all which are urged there as reasons for the humility, modesty, silence, and submissiveness, of that sex in general, and particularly the subjection and reverence which wives owe to their own husbands. Yet, man being made last of the creatures, as the best and most excellent of all, Eve's being made after Adam, and out of him, puts an honor upon that sex, as the glory of man, if man is the head, she is the crown, a crown to her husband, the crown of the visible creation. The man was dust refined, but the woman was dust double refined.*[24]

---

http://www.hebrew4christians.com/Names_of_G-d/Spirit_of_God/spirit_ot_god.html.
[23] Fretheim, *God and World in the Old Testament*, 56.
[24] Henry, *Matthew Henry's Commentary on the Whole Bible*, 78.

Additionally, Henry demonstrates the importance of a woman in a man's life and how they work together in union to glorify God. He goes on further to state:

> *The woman was made of a rib out of the side of Adam; not made out of his head to rule over him, nor out of his feet to be trampled upon by him, but out of his side to be equal to him, under his arm to be protected, and near his heart to be beloved.*[25]

Throughout Scripture, admonitions against hostility towards our partners are apparent. The Apostle Peter tells us, *"Husbands, in the same way be considerate as you live with your wives and treat them with respect as the weaker partner and as heirs with you of the gracious gift of life, so that nothing will hinder your prayers."*[26]

I once had an Old Testament History and Poetry professor give a charge to one of my colleagues on his wedding day. In the charge, he emphasized trusting in God's design.[27] I couldn't help but think to myself, how true. God designed our relationship to Him and each other faultlessly. When we try and create our own design of various gods that we want to build relationships with, or which self-identifying partner we try and be intimate with, we are working contrary to God's design, and it's going to have ramifications.

God has been active in a triune sense from the beginning of time. Note that in Chapter one of Genesis, God says, *"Let us make mankind in our image"*[28] denoting that the Trinitarian relational God was present at mankind's creation. God creates mankind and forms a relationship with Him. Then, God created woman out of man to have a relationship with both God, and with each other.

The theme of Genesis chapter two is the climax of God's creation. Adam and Eve were commissioned as representatives to fill the earth and govern the other creatures. The goal is to show that there was a time in

---

[25] Ibid.
[26] 1 Pet 3:7 (NIV).
[27] Professor Jay Hull, Josh Roebuck's Wedding, January 9, 2017.
[28] Gen 1:26 (NIV).

which Yahweh walked in the garden alongside His creation in a perfect relationship. The fall broke that relationship, though not entirely. When Adam went into hiding after his trespass, the ever-omniscient God was not asking where was Adam physically, but rather, where was Adam *relationally*?

The meaning of Genesis two in the context of the entire Bible is to show that God intended for mankind to dwell in the garden eternally in perfect relationship with Him. Due to Adam choosing to become his own god at the fall, that relationship was severed. However, a severed relationship is not an amputated one. In fact, despite the justification God would have had to cut off His people completely due to their disobedience, His grace demonstrated quite the opposite. Prior to the Fall, trusting in God's design ensured happiness. This passage tells us about God and His will for a loving relationship with Adam and Eve. God warns Adam and Eve of the consequences of disobedience should they allow temptation to take hold.

In God's creation of mankind, we see the first covenant established between God and Adam, and ultimately the rejection of that covenant. The Israelites reading Moses' book of Genesis would have realized the relationship God was trying to have with His creation, as well as the consequences of distancing themselves from that relationship through their sin. "And the LORD God commanded the man, saying, 'Of every tree of the garden you may freely eat; but of the tree of the knowledge of good and evil you shall not eat, for in the day that you eat of it you shall surely die."[29] This was the covenant made between God and Adam. The covenant consists of several positive commands because man (both male and female) was created in God's image:

- Man was to subdue the earth.
- Man was given dominion and authority over the earth and the animal kingdom.
- Mankind was to reproduce and inhabit the entire earth.
- Man was also to keep the garden sanctuary.
- The covenant consisted of one negative command.

---

[29] Gen. 2:16–17 (New King James Version).

11

God had given Adam and Eve great responsibility while in the Garden. The naming of the animals significantly demonstrates just how much God trusted Adam and Eve. In his book, *God and World in The Old Testament,* Dr. Fretheim makes this relational connection:

> *The human beings' naming of each creature is meant to parallel to the divine naming in Genesis chapter 1, verses 5-10. This act is not a perfunctory utilitarian move, a labeling of the cages of the world zoo. Naming is a part of the creative process itself, discerning the very nature of intra-creaturely relationships. Human decisions are shown to be important in the ongoing development of the created order. It is not that human beings have the capacity to stymie God's movement into the future in any final way, but God has established a relationship with human beings such that their decisions about the creation truly count.*[30]

The one prohibition given to Adam and Eve was not to eat of the tree of good and evil. Although Adam was made in the very image of God and had delegated authority from God over creation, he was to remember that he was subservient to God and incapable of determining good and evil. The penalty for breaking this command was death.[31] We know that God viewed these commands as a covenant because of how He viewed Adam's fall; *"But like Adam they have transgressed the covenant; There they have dealt treacherously against Me."*[32]

God has always been restorative. When Jesus Christ made mud from the earth and placed it on the blind man's eyes in John chapter nine, He was restoring the man to the completed state of Adam in the garden. Just as the Father formed Adam from the ground, Jesus restored sight with God's soil. Ultimately, God will restore all of creation with the new heavens and new earth. Just as creation once was, in perfect harmony with the Father, God will ultimately restore everything to the pre-fallen state at the end of time. Wheaton College Professor of Old Testament, Sandra Richter, notes:

---

[30] Fretheim, *God and World in the Old Testament,* 58.
[31] Whitefield, "The Adamic Covenant," Samuel Whitefield.com, March 22, 2013, https://samuelwhitefield.com/591/the-adamic-covenant.
[32] Hos. 6:7 (New American Standard Bible).

> *What began in Eden, ends in Eden. God's original intent to offer kingdom citizenship to every man, woman, and child has been re-accomplished in Christ. God's original plan that the children of Adam might build their city in the midst of his kingdom is recreated in the new earth. His driving desire to be with us is fulfilled as the Presence that walked in the garden now illuminates the New Jerusalem.*[33]

In Christ Jesus, all things are made new. The Light had ushered in the beginning of this restoration process by proclaiming that the kingdom of heaven was at hand.[34] John 1:14 tells us, *"And the Word became flesh and dwelt among us."*[35] Much like God dwelt with Adam and Eve in the Garden, Jesus dwelt among the people of the 1st century; teaching them, healing them, communing with them, tabernacling among them, and restoring them.

Jesus Christ is the living Word and He still dwells among us today in the form of the Holy Spirit. God continues His relationship with His creation now through our faith in His only begotten Son. In the fullness of time, God will join us again in paradise as His Son rules over us day and night. Our relationship with the Father will endure as it did from our time in the garden like a never-ending circle.

God promised that if man ate of the tree of knowledge, he would surely die. That promise was fulfilled at the Fall since at some point, we will all die. A part of Adam died spiritually that day as well. Yet, there is hope in a future restoration through Jesus Christ. The Apostle Paul tells us, *"But if Christ is in you, then even though your body is subject to death because of sin, the Spirit gives life because of righteousness."*[36]

Post-fall, we were shielded from God's presence. Yet, God's son removed that shield from our eyes. God, Himself, is a pre-figure of Christ because God and Christ are one. Jesus Christ is the incarnate God. Both continue in relationship with us through the Holy Spirit. By analogy, this passage shows us who God in Christ is for us today. The death of Jesus Christ marked a new beginning. No longer does the veil shield God from His creation. Now that veil is torn, allowing us to experience God face-to-

---

[33] Richter, *The Epic of Eden,* 224.
[34] See Matt. 4:12-17.
[35] John 1:14 (NIV).
[36] Rom. 8:10 (NIV).

face. The relational theme of Genesis chapter two tracks from the Old Testament into the New Testament. We can see how God intends on restoring the perfect relationship He started, in the new heavens and new earth.

A few years ago, I took a Hebrews through Revelation course and the professor[37] of the course told us to read the following books and chapters in this order:

Genesis 3
Revelation 20
Genesis 2
Revelation 21
Genesis 1
Revelation 22

It's amazing how God reinstates His creation back to the way it was originally envisioned, and it's all revealed to us in Scripture itself! For example, Genesis 2:9 states that *"Out of the ground the Lord God caused to grow every tree that is pleasing to the sight and good for food; the tree of life also in the midst of the garden, and the tree of the knowledge of good and evil."*[38] Yet in Revelation 22:2, there is no longer a tree of the knowledge of good and evil, but rather, a tree of healing: *"In the middle of its street. On either side of the river was the tree of life, bearing twelve kinds of fruit, yielding its fruit every month; and the leaves of the tree were for the healing of the nations."*[39]

One can see how God restores the disunity of the nations through the tree of life. This unity is what the body of Christ represents. According to Christian psychologist, Christina Cleveland, "To embrace our identities in this new, Christian family, we must engage in the difficult process of lessening our grip on the identities that we have idolized and clung to for far too long."[40]

There is a contrast between the relationship of Adam and Eve to God in Genesis chapter two, and their relationship with God post-fall. Fear, separation, and shame enter the conscience of Adam and Eve after their trans-

---

[37] Professor Bill Osgood, Hebrews through Revelation Class, January 22, 2016.
[38] Gen. 2:9 (NASB).
[39] Rev. 22:2 (NASB).
[40] Cleveland, *Disunity in Christ*, 189.

gression. God's relationship extends to mankind despite our rebellion against Him. One goal of Genesis chapter two was to create Adam and Eve so that they could live in a loving relationship with God. Isaiah 43:7 tells us that *"everyone who is called by God's name was created for His glory."*[41] Therefore, the ultimate purpose of man, according to the Bible, is simply to glorify God. Yet, to fulfill that purpose, we must live our lives in relationship and faithfulness to Him.

John Piper once asked, "Did Christ die for us or for God?"[42] A profound question, indeed. The truth is, Christ died for God's glory; remaining obedient to Him unto death upon the cross.[43] We have the gift of salvation as a result of Christ glorifying God in such a way. God's love for us is unconditional and is a love that kept Christ on the cross; whereas, our love for Him can often be quite fickle.

Shame is a psychological cancer that eats away at our very being. Once, many thousands of years ago, shame entered into creation immediately following the Fall. Once Adam and Eve felt shame, they immediately clothed themselves and hid from God.[44] The effects of shame have been felt in our culture ever since the deception of the Evil One.

Dr. Curt Thompson, in his book, *Anatomy of the Soul*, defines shame as, "Being separated or disconnected from God or behaviors that lead to that condition."[45] In relation, the Hebrew and Greek words for sin both describe it as "missing the mark." Sin, does indeed, reinforce the idea of missing the mark which leads to feelings of shame and guilt. Thompson further expands upon sin in a psychological sense as *disconnection* or *disintegration*.[46]

Shame can be self-destructive. Brené Brown, in her book, *Rising Strong*, defines shame as focusing on ourselves,[47] or a negative experience in which we internalize our feelings to the point of equating our experience with our

---

[41] Is. 43:7 (NIV).

[42] Piper, *Reading the Bible Supernaturally*, 49.

[43] See Phil. 2:8.

[44] Gen. 3:7-8 (Emphasis mine).

[45] Thompson, *Anatomy of the Soul*, 183.

[46] Ibid.

[47] Brown, *Rising Strong*, 194.

state of being. She also contrasts guilt as focusing on our behavior.[48] Brown further states that shame and comparison are partners in crime because we often shame ourselves by comparing ourselves to other people.[49]

Shame and guilt overlap, and of course, both occur because we are in a broken world with sin abounding in it. Without sin, one could argue, there would be no shame or guilt. Brown gives a good illustration of the psychological effects of shame when she gives the example of, "I screwed up" (guilt statement) vs. "I *am* a screwup" (shame statement).[50]

Shame affects us psychologically, emotionally, and spiritually. There are several instances in which I found myself separating from God because of the shame I was experiencing from an act or event that took place in my life. In a presentation on shame, Christian Counseling professor, Dr. Barbara Feil, notes:

> *We are disappointed as victims and culpable as agents who experience guilt and shame. We have been sinned against and we continue to be injured by other's sin and we continue to sin deepening our guilt and shame. To deal with guilt and shame we consciously but more often unconsciously continue to work at preserving our life with defensive patterns of relating that actually perpetuate the cycle of sin and shame.[51]*

This is where shame involves a cycle of disobedience towards God and each other. By using these defensive patterns to inflict our pain on others, we not only hurt them but hurt ourselves in the process.

In an insightful TED talk by Dr. Brené Brown, vulnerability is highlighted as a means in which we sometimes experience shame, yet can also be the birthplace of joy, creativity, and love. Brown notes that shame is the fear of disconnection.[52] I feel that in this sense, vulnerability does not have to lead to shameful feelings as long as we are confident in our self-worth and value. If I am confident in my standing before God, then I can use vul-

---

[48] Ibid.
[49] Ibid., 195.
[50] Ibid., 194.
[51] Dr. Feil, PowerPoint Presentation on Sin, Guilt, and Shame (Slide 9), September 26, 2019.
[52] Brown, "The Power of Vulnerability," TEDx Houston, January 3, 2011, https://www.youtube.com/watch?v=iCvmsMzlF7o.

nerability to combat shame because I can come to a place before others where I am dependent upon them for their human connection, regardless if I come across as needy or insecure.

Reflecting upon my own shame, I would say that it stems from my insecurities about myself from words used by my stepfather that made me feel like I wasn't smart enough, or that I couldn't contribute to dinner-table conversations in a fact-based manner. Often, he would use sarcasm to put down what I was saying or excited to share. Those experiences of shame still come back to haunt me. Two things helped me to combat those feelings: 1) I now only discuss topics that I have vast amounts of knowledge in or topics that I'm certain my stepfather does not have more knowledge than me in, and 2) I have been able to forgive my stepfather for his hurtful words, knowing that he experienced some of the same psychological hardships from his own father.

The gospel message speaks hope into a shameful state of being. Jesus Christ has conquered sin and death on the cross; therefore, we are no longer prisoners to our sinful thoughts, or the behaviors of others—for we are now new creations in Christ.[53] Knowing this helps me in my ministry because I now empathize with others who have experienced shame at some point in their lives. Being able to relate to people on a human level, going along with them on their journey through life, and hearing what they are saying, actually helps in many ways to deal with my shame and guilt.

I once experienced a feeling of shame after scoring only an eighty percent on a Greek quiz and a seventy percent on a subsequent quiz. It sounds silly because they were collectively only weighted at twenty percent of our total grade, and I was really in no danger of failing the course. The "old man" from my past sometimes creeps his head up and says things like,

> *Everyone is depending on you for help; How can you tutor students in Greek when you can't even score an A on your own quizzes?; If you don't score better, you'll lower your overall GPA of 3.98 and risk not getting Summa Cum Laude at graduation.*

---

[53] 2 Cor. 5:17 (Emphasis mine).

17

Do you see how Satan can turn guilt into shame quite easily? Besides, is it my goal to impress God, or to impress man? This is why we must always be on guard spiritually. Satan does not attack us with flesh, but with the spiritual forces of this dark world.[54]

Though shame may alter our mindset about our self-worth, we must always realize that we do not live our lives by the world's standards; we live our lives by God's standards. God gives us our value and worth and loves us unconditionally. This belief gives us confidence that we will always emerge victorious during any spiritual battle through the power of the Holy Spirit.

In stark contrast to feeling shame, we can be confident that God loves us very much. In fact, so much, that He sent His only son to die for our sins so that we might not perish but enjoy eternal life.[55] Many of us have children or grandchildren. Think of how involved we are in their lives every single day. That is how intricately God the Father is involved in our lives. Author, Ian Coate, gives a great illustration involving a relationship that contrasts religion with Christianity. Coate states:

> *For most, business and pleasure are not the same things. When asked: 'Are you here for business or pleasure?' people often mean: 'Are you here because you have to be or want to be?' Christianity was designed to be a wonderful relationship with God—not a religion. Sadly, the greatest obstacle for many people coming to Christianity is religion. It has turned what should be a pleasure into a business. Religion, burdened with its numerous works, rituals, cults, intolerance, and atrocities, has distorted the true meaning of Christianity. God isn't interested in religion—He doesn't need our insignificant works or our meagre money to complete His purpose, (Ephesians 2:8-9). He is God, the Creator of the universe—Governor of the laws that sustain science—Possessor of all knowledge and riches. God doesn't need our help—we need His. God is like a loving parent whose children have run away. His greatest desire is for us to choose to come back to Him. God created mankind with free will. He cannot and will not force anyone to love Him. We are created in His image—just as we desire people to freely love us, so too does God want us to freely love Him. God desires a personal relationship with each of us. As a parent, He*

---

[54] Eph. 6:10-12 (Emphasis mine).
[55] John 3:16 (Emphasis mine).

*wants to protect and provide for us. He wants to impart His wisdom. His rules are written not to spoil our chance at happiness, but to increase it. Christianity is not a set of meaningless rituals, but a restoration of a family relationship with our Heavenly Father.*[56]

Just as the absence of sin allowed Adam and Eve to have a perfect relationship with God in the Garden, we too can have a perfect relationship with God by resisting sin. But this takes faith. Faith in Jesus Christ who overcame sin and conquered death; Jesus is the second Adam. Because we cannot conquer our demons on our own, we must work on building our relationship with Jesus Christ to emerge victorious.

We can all step towards Jesus Christ by taking time out to pray regularly, share the gospel message, read the living Word, and trust in what God has called each one of us to do to help build up His kingdom. Then, we can start getting to really know Him as He knew and loved us before the foundation of the world. We should be working on a relationship with God and conforming to Christlikeness out of gratitude for God's grace, not in obligation to it.

*Earthly Relationships*

Forming a relationship with God is relatively easy because Jesus Christ can be, and is, both Lord and friend. Not to mention, He already knows every hair on our heads.[57] However, forming genuine relationships with other human beings, made in His image, is not so easy. Jesus once said, "But I say to you who hear, love your enemies, do good to those who curse you, pray for those who abuse you."[58] Not only should we lovingly relate to our enemies, but we should also be devoted to one another, honor one another, live in harmony with one another, and build up one another.[59] This is why God's unconditional love is so powerful. We experience love from Him and can then share His love with others.

---

[56] Coate, "Christianity: Business or Pleasure?" Relationship Illustrations, Free Christian Illustrations, accessed October 23, 2017,
http://www.freechristianillustrations.com/relationships.html.
[57] Luke 12:7 (Emphasis mine).
[58] Luke 6:27-28 (ESV).
[59] See Rom. 12:10; 16, Rom. 14:19.

I once used social media to reach out to someone who had hurt me many years ago. I told him that I forgave him for any pain or suffering that he caused me and that I was praying for him and his family. His response brought tears to my eyes. He said that he, too, was bullied at a young age and was so sorry for anything that he had done to me. He said that he wanted to use my message to teach his own children that it's wrong to bully people and that even people who make poor decisions deserve forgiveness. What a powerful experience for us both. God is teaching us the importance of love and is at work doing so at all times; if we would just listen to what His Spirit has to say to us.

Aside from loving our enemies, it's sometimes challenging to love someone who acts or looks different than us. This especially holds true when dealing with mental health issues in the church. Mental health concerns within the modern church are on the rise. According to the National Institute of Mental Health, nine percent of all adults exhibit some kind of personality disorder.[60]

Long ago, when I was just beginning my theological academic journey, one of my Spiritual Formation professors said:

*We have a lot of programs for people in the church. If you are struggling with addiction, there's a program for you. If you have questions about doctrine or church polity, there's a program for you. If you have trouble finding dates to go on with like-minded, spiritual people, there's a program for you. Yet, when it comes to mental health issues, or people with disabilities, the church does a poor job of offering a program to help deal or cope with people who fall into that category, of which, my own daughter is one.*[61]

It was then that I realized that he was right. Out of the various churches that I'd attended in the past thirty years (even going back to 1986), there wasn't one that I could remember that offered a mental health ministry or outreach program; this includes Non-denominational, Charismatic, Lutheran, Presbyterian, and Pentecostal denominations.

---

[60] Simpson, *Troubled Minds*, 50.
[61] Dr. McKendricks, Spiritual Formation I Lecture, September 2014.

According to Sharon Johnson, mental health breaks down into the following categories: Infancy Disorders (such as mental retardation, PDD, and ADHD), Organic Mental Syndromes (such as Alzheimer's or Dementia), Substance Abuse Disorders (including oral, injection, snorting, and inhaling), Psychotic Disorders (such as schizophrenia), Mood Disorders (such as Bipolar and Depression), Anxiety Disorders (including PTSD and panic attacks), Somatoform Disorders (which are primarily physiological in nature), and Dissociative, Sexual, Adjustment, Impulse Control, and Personality Disorders.[62] After reviewing this laundry list of disorders, I was confident that I had at least one or two.

The church is obligated to address these types of issues if we are truly loving our neighbors as ourselves. Mental illness, toxic faith, sexuality and gender, addictions, broken marriages, and abuses (sexual, emotional, physical, and spiritual) all exist amongst our parishioners, both in and outside of the church walls. As Dr. Barbara Feil dually notes, "Our disconnection from God, creation, and each other, are all a result of the Fall."[63]

As members of Christ's church, we need to be willing participants involving God's plan of redemption by being there for one another during the restoration process. Broken marriages are all too common. If we realize that a covenant relationship involves more of a commitment to the process, rather than yielding the product of that process (happiness), then surely, we can overcome the everyday obstacles Satan uses to separate us.[64] Our challenge is that we cannot return to the way things once were, but we can respond with love in sharing the Gospel of Jesus Christ, which has worked for over two-thousand years in restoring people to a place of right-standing before the Father.[65]

All of us are broken. None of us can re-order our sexual desires but we have this God who has given us—through the power of His Holy Spir-

---

[62] Johnson, "Therapist Guide to Clinical Intervention," PowerPoint Presentation, The website for NIMH – National Institute for Mental Health, 2004,
https://www.nimh.nih.gov/index.shtml.
[63] Dr. Feil, "Sorting out a Biblical Response to Gender and Sexuality in our World Today," PowerPoint Presentation, slide 4, accessed October 1, 2019,
https://learn.multnomah.edu/courses/590//files/286800?module_item_id=105806.
[64] Ibid., 7.
[65] Ibid., 32-33.

it—everything we need to live a self-controlled, godly, relationally rich, holy life in the middle of a crooked and depraved generation.[66] Indeed, through the ultimate power of the Holy Spirit, we can control our sinful urges, repent of them, and live sexually healthy and productive lives.

The church is the first place that many people go when they are in a crisis. We, as pastors, must get help for ourselves if we are struggling in a mental health area. I struggled with depression in my early childhood and teen years. I sought out a family therapist who could help me overcome my insecurities from my past. Perhaps, of equal or more value, I pursued help in my local church from mentors and church leaders who spent time with me sharing the gospel message and encouraging me to remain strong in the Holy Spirit.

We should share our own story with others who may be struggling with a similar mental health issue. Vulnerability is a huge asset when we relate to, or formally council, someone within a church setting. But, please always remember that our job is not to solve all of their problems. Our job is to go on the journey with them.[67] By empathizing and sharing relatable stories, the counseled will feel as though we are holding their pain and anxiety with them, or in other words, we are making an intimate human connection that they so desperately need.

Some other ways to help someone with mental challenges include getting educated in mental health, de-stigmatizing the mental health culture, asking for other ways we can help, and talking about mental illness during small groups or in sermons.[68] These are all great methods in which churches and church leaders can help to address mental health and suspend judgment at the same time.

Even our best intentions in caring for the mental health of our church members have limits. Simpson rightly notes that we should draw boundaries and know when we are in over our heads.[69] I remember during my Introduction to Counseling course at the undergraduate level, Professor Katy

---

[66] Ibid., 45.
[67] Dr. Feil, Counseling 721 Online Lecture, September 11, 2019.
[68] Simpson, *Troubled Minds*, 181-184.
[69] Ibid., 190-191.

Hartley (*MFT, LSW*) used to tell us that whenever we feel uncomfortable with a counseling session, we should refer out. For this reason, I've kept an updated referral list of licensed therapists (both Christian and non-Christian) that I can, and have, sent to those counseled.

As already noted, one way that we can address these issues is in sermons and teachings. By discussing the tough theological questions that mental illness raises, establishing our church community as imperfect people growing in a relationship with God, and avoiding labels, we can avoid the ramifications of toxic faith systems in which judgment, perfect people, and stigmatism thrive and flourish.[70]

Another way to engage leaders in the area of mental health is to have them attend counseling courses either online or at a Bible College. I've learned a lot about pastoral care, soul care, and Christian counseling just from the few courses I've had at Multnomah University. By no means have I perfected the art and science of Christian counseling, but I have added some valuable tools to my toolbox that I didn't have before—thanks to formal Christian education.

An inordinate way to help battle sexual, mental, and emotional addiction is through spiritual formation. Through prayer, meditation, time in solitude with the Father, reading Scripture, spending time with others in the faith who have similar challenges, and working out our salvation, we can add an extra hedge of protection against the powers and spiritual forces of evil which exist on this earth.[71] I've personally experienced the Holy Spirit blocking possible sins from occurring in my own life simply by spending time in prayer to God, asking Him to protect me from the temptations of the day.

Discipleship can aid with our mental challenges as well. As Solomon rightly says, *"Iron sharpens Iron, and one man sharpens another."*[72] By reading, studying, and meditating on God's Word with another brother or sister in the faith, we can begin to overcome our depression or insecurities and real-

---

[70] Ibid., 182.
[71] Eph. 6:10-16 (Emphasis mine).
[72] Prov. 27:17 (English Standard Version).

ize that we are fully redeemed in God's eyes through the blood sacrifice of Jesus Christ.

Lastly, it's important to utilize available community resources. Through pastoral councilors, licensed therapists, and other vital mental health resources, we can collectively battle mental health conditions and help in the restoration and healing process. We, as a church body and society, need to de-stigmatize the use of medicine to help in the healing process. God certainly oversees chemists and physicians who spend their lives studying ways to heal the mind, so taking prescription medication in addition to pastoral care should be more acceptable in our society.

Whether we are interacting with someone that has mental challenges or interacting with someone of sound mind, we must love them regardless because they are made in God's image. The latter half of the great commandment involves

loving our neighbor as ourselves.[73] Who is our neighbor? The person next door? The person addicted to drugs? The rich man? The poor man? The successful man? The sexually addicted man? Our neighbor is anyone and everyone. Love them and you will be fulfilling half of God's great commandment.[74]

*Prayer of Relationship*

Heavenly Father, Lord of our hearts. You see us, you know us, you love us, and protect us. I pray that You will bless our relationship and lift us up in service to You as Christians and as the people You want us to be. I ask that your Holy Spirit sanctify us both individually, and as a whole for the joy of working together to glorify You and Your church. Lord, show us the path to service, heal any fractures in our relationship now or in the future, and build a hedge of protection around us, to guard us against outside forces that might try to attack us. Make this a godly, righteous relationship

---

[73] Matt. 22:39 (Emphasis mine).
[74] The Parable of the Good Samaritan is only found in Luke's Gospel and strongly elaborates upon Jesus' position of how to treat one another. This is especially true with those whom were considered enemies to the Israelites and those that were considered less than adequate within the class system of the first century. Jesus often spoke in parables to convey a broader moral message in a culturally relevant context. See Luke 10:25-37.

for loving and serving You and Your chosen people. I thank You, Lord, for the faith You've given me to know that this is true—that You protect, You guard, You guide, and You love us. In Jesus' Name. Amen![75]

*Conclusion*

In this chapter, we've covered how sin separates us from a healthy relationship with the Father. We've also discovered the importance of working towards perfection in Christ through progressive sanctification and the spiritual disciplines. We went over God's relationship to His creation as demonstrated in the first three chapters of Genesis, and how that relationship is continued today. Lastly, we considered how we can relate better to each other, and discussed some of the challenges that the church faces today regarding mental health.

After years of backsliding, challenges, triumphs, learning about God and myself, and teaching and preaching God's Word, I've come to realize that I'm only a fraction of where I want to—or could—be in my quest for spiritual formation and growth. We never stop growing.

---

[75] Adaptation of: "Prayer Power," Word Press, accessed October 23, 2017, http://prayer-power.com/prayer-relationships/.

# CHAPTER 2

## Spiritual Formation Throughout the Ages

There are a few prominent divisions within Christian theology that should be defined and elaborated upon. Therefore, I'd like to take a few moments to share with you some of the characteristics that are unique to each division. The following are some of the differences and parallels between Systematic Theology, Biblical Theology, and Spiritual Theology.

Defining "theology" is best accomplished when the word is broken out into its etymological segments. The Greek word, θεός is translated into English as "God." The Greek word λόγος is translated into English as "Word" or "Reasoning." Finally, the word "ology" is "the study of." Theology literally means *the study of God's Word*, or *the study of God's reasoning*.[76] I must take care in qualifying the term "Christian Theology." The word, *God*, can serve as a higher being in other religious belief systems, in addition to Christianity. When I use the term, *theology*, I am using it in respect to a trinitarian Christian world view.

Systematic theology can be defined as any study that answers the question of: *What does the whole Bible teach us today about any given topic?* Systematic theology includes the understanding of all the relevant passages in the Bible on various topics and then summarizing and categorizing their teachings clearly so that we know what to believe about each topic.[77]

---

[76] Professor Slavin, Theology I, personal correspondence, January 2014.

[77] Grudem, *Systematic Theology*, 21.

Systematic theology tends to compartmentalize or "systematize" certain doctrines extrapolated from Scripture into learnable topics or categories. Examples of these categories include: Anthropology, Theology Proper, Bibliology, Angelology, Soteriology, Ecclesiology, Eschatology, Pneumatology, Christology, et al.

Biblical theology can be described as the study of seeking, uncovering, and articulating the unity of all the biblical texts taken together—resorting primarily to the categories of those texts themselves. Biblical theology is particularly concerned with the diverse literary and historical contexts of the story. Lastly, biblical theology attempts to relate the meaning of the story in terms of the story itself.[78]

In contrast to systematic theology, biblical theology concentrates its efforts in discovering biblical truths, narratives, and meta-narratives, as they develop chronologically throughout Scripture. Systematic theology has less regard for a biblical timetable, and instead draws its doctrines from a variety of Scriptures in an attempt to categorize them, regardless of their placement within the Bible. A true biblical theologian does not feel too compelled to address or answer issues not clearly stated in the text; whereas, systematic theologians are more inclined to "fill in the blanks." The systematic theologian assumes a controlling posture in holding to certain doctrines, while the biblical theologian is more comfortable with saying "I don't know about ____; the Bible does not address that,"—whatever it may be.[79]

Some examples of biblical theology could be the order of creation, fall, redemption, and restoration as they unfold throughout the Scriptures; focusing on how those truths relate to us as Christ-followers, and how collectively, those theological actualities culminate in God's plan of redemption for all of creation through His Son, Jesus Christ.

Spiritual theology can be expressed in a way all theological reflections ought to be conveyed. Spiritual theology is a distinct branch of theological

---

[78] Carson, *New Dictionary of Biblical Theology*, 100.
[79] Dr. Blom, Spiritual Theology, personal correspondence, April 28, 2020.

study that is concerned with the principles and practices of the Christian life.[80]

Spiritual theology differs from both systematic and biblical theology in the sense that it is more personal and relational in scope and practice. Spiritual theology defines the nature of the supernatural life, formulates directives for personal growth and development (particularly regarding sin and temptation), and explains the process by which souls advance from the beginning, to perfection or glorification in Christ.[81]

All of these disciplines interface with each other in some form. The study of God's Word involves, not only knowing the doctrines and principles contained within Holy Scripture but also living them out in pragmatic and relational ways. Spiritual theology encompasses exercises such as focusing on God and self, focusing on the Word, and the discerning of spirits, prayer, and spiritual direction.

Systematic and biblical theology help us to categorize biblical doctrines and truths as they appear in Scripture and to realize the meta-narrative of the Bible which answers the questions of: *Who is God? What does He desire from us?* And, *What is His plan of redemption for us?* The theme of love runs throughout the Bible; therefore, we should also love God in our endeavors to get to know Him better through theology.

*Historical Christian Spirituality*

Historical Christian spirituality has many aspects and schools of thought to it. From its Jewish roots to the New Testament period, the Monastics to the Middle Ages, to Byzantine spirituality and the modern period, there is continuity and uniformity, but also nuanced and subtle variations that appear throughout the ages. Author, Urban T. Holmes III, has an excellent book, *A History of Christian Spirituality*, that I will utilize as a source text for my thoughts and annotations on historical Christian spirituality.

Most spiritual formation studies contain a perspective on prayer. I cover prayer in a later chapter, so I won't go into much detail here; howev-

---

[80] Chan, *Spiritual Theology*, 16.
[81] Ibid., 18.

er, I wanted to include some insights on prayer to sort of "prime the pump" in an effort to help motivate one into looking into the study and practice of prayer in more depth. In reference to prayer, Holmes states, "For us, to pray is to intend to hear God and to respond to God. God is absolutely present to all people. Prayer does not make him present…It begins with our consent to enter into a relationship to which God invites everyone."[82]

This is a stark reminder that 1) God is relational and we must engage in that relationship. And, 2) Prayer does not guarantee the result that we desire. Sometimes the answer is *no*; sometimes the answer is *yes*; and sometimes, the answer is *not yet*. When we pray, we are not asking God for a Christmas wish list. When we pray, we are thanking God for what He's already planned to do in our lives.

We must also remember that it is not God who changes, it is we who change and the way we understand God from our finite perspective that changes.[83] The reality is, God is God, and we are not. He is beyond our complete understanding, yet we can begin to appreciate Him better by engaging in a relationship with Him through prayer, meditation, and several other facets of spiritual formation. Heaven and earth will pass away, yet God's words are unchanging, and will never pass away.[84]

Holmes describes a dichotomy of the phenomenology of prayer; being either *apophatic* (emptying meditation) or *kataphatic* (imaginative meditation).[85] There is somewhat of a juxtaposition of both during prayer; I personally prefer the apophatic method when I pray. I choose this method because I feel that it has the best chance of allowing the Spirit of God to enter into my mind and heart, unconstrained by my flesh. Have you ever started with a wonderful prayer only to be distracted by your thoughts having some vulgar or ungodly image come to mind? That's the flesh, and Satan using our flesh against us. Rebuke him and continue to pray in the Spirit. God surely knows your heart. Now, we'll take a look at the more notorious schools of spiritual theology as they have developed throughout history.

---

[82] Holmes III, *A History of Christian Spirituality*, 2.
[83] Ibid.
[84] See Matt. 24:35.
[85] Holmes III, *A History of Christian Spirituality*, 4.

*Jewish Spirituality*

Historically, early Christianity was not referred to as Christianity at all. Rather, it was referred to as a movement called, "The Way." The term "Christian" was a derogatory one used by the Romans to refer to a first-century sect of Judaism.[86] The Jews regarded the *Shekinah* glory as the manifestation of God in the early Jewish community. The Shekinah can be paralleled to God's radiant glory shining through even the darkest times; like the sun's rays shining from behind a dark cloud.[87]

Sadly, mysticism had influenced certain Jewish sects.[88] Historically, both mysticism and Gnosticism had manipulated early converts to Christianity, as well as, had an impact on the Jewish community prior to Jesus' incarnation. Philo, a Jewish Hellenistic philosopher who lived during the time of Jesus, may well have been the father of both pagan and Christian mysticism. Philo contended that the Spirit of God takes the place in the humanity of our spirit; in the mind.[89]

Many ancient philosophers contended that the mind and soul were one. This line of thought does seem to have support when reading Pauline literature (see Rom. 12:2). However, Paul tends to delineate the terms spirit, soul, and body in many of his writings. This separation argues in favor of the notion that humankind is tripartite. It is interesting that when you look at various translations of 1 Thessalonians 5:23, commas are placed incongruously. Are the commas located after spirit, and soul, and body? Or, is the comma only after soul, in which spirit and soul are connected as one in the same entity? Or, perhaps, the comma is only after spirit, connecting the soul and body? The ESV (and several other formal translations) seems to stay true to the Greek in which there was no punctuation during the koine period: *"Now may the God of peace himself sanctify you completely and may your whole spirit and soul and body be kept blameless at the coming of our Lord Jesus Christ."*[90]

*Alexandrian Spirituality*

---

[86] Gonzalez, *The Story of Christianity*, 40-42
[87] Holmes III, *A History of Christian Spirituality*, 15.
[88] Ibid., 16.
[89] Ibid., 17.
[90] 1 Thess. 5:23 (ESV).

The Alexandrian school's development of Christian Spirituality was somewhat syncretistic. They blended Neo-Platonism philosophical concepts with orthodox teachings. Ironically, this is the same type of heresy that led to the condemnation of Origen's theology in the 6th century at the Synod of Constantinople. One should caution against promoting any type of platonic philosophy within Christianity. Receiving the "Gnosis" as a gift from God is not limited to certain enlightened thinkers. Rather, it's given to all who accept Jesus Christ into their hearts, for we all have the same Spirit and do not require an enlightened teacher (see 1 Cor. 12:13; 1 John 2:27). Similarly, an unknown god cannot give knowledge and should not be worshiped. The Apostle Paul explains that the "unknown god" can indeed be known:

*A group of Epicurean and Stoic philosophers began to debate with him. Some of them asked, 'What is this babbler trying to say?' Others remarked, 'He seems to be advocating foreign gods.' They said this because Paul was preaching the good news about Jesus and the resurrection. Then they took him and brought him to a meeting of the Areopagus, where they said to him, 'May we know what this new teaching is that you are presenting? You are bringing some strange ideas to our ears, and we would like to know what they mean.' (All the Athenians and the foreigners who lived there spent their time doing nothing but talking about and listening to the latest ideas.)*

*Paul then stood up in the meeting of the Areopagus and said: 'People of Athens! I see that in every way you are very religious. For as I walked around and looked carefully at your objects of worship, I even found an altar with this inscription: to an unknown god. So, you are ignorant of the very thing you worship—and this is what I am going to proclaim to you.'*

*The God who made the world and everything in it is the Lord of heaven and earth and does not live in temples built by human hands. And he is not served by human hands, as if he needed anything. Rather, he himself gives everyone life and breath and everything else. From one man he made all the nations, that they should inhabit the whole earth; and he marked out their appointed times in history and the boundaries of their lands. God did this so that they would seek him and perhaps reach out for him and find him, though he is not far from any one of us. 'For in him we live and move and have our being. 'As some of your own poets have said, 'We are his offspring.'*[91]

One of the more prominent philosophers and theologians during the Alexandrian period was Origen. I took a Patristics course about a year ago and wrote my final paper on Origen of Alexandria. Origen had some good theological positions, but also had some heretical ones.

He was one of the first people to publicly define Mary's role in the incarnation as Θεοτόκος "God-bearer," a position that was later elevated to "Eternal Virgin" at the Council of Constantinople.[92] He loved Jesus but was too liberal with allegorical interpretation. One sure method of interpreting Scripture is to let the Scripture interpret itself with other Scripture. There are allegorical Scriptures, (see most of Jesus' parables, 1 Cor. 10:4, Gal. 4:21-31) but the only allegory that is sound academically is when it can be backed up by another biblical author.

*Monastic Spirituality*

The monastics practiced a life in solitude. In fact, the term "anchoritism" or "anchorite" means withdrawn.[93] According to Holmes, there were two forms of anchorite life: eremitical, meaning life totally in solitude; and cenobitical, meaning participants gathered in the community each day.[94] Biblically, cenobitical anchoritism holds more weight. Jesus indeed withdrew regularly to pray to the Father in solitude, but He didn't remain in solitude because the whole point of the Ecclesia (*church*), is to gather together.[95]

There was a third-century anchorite, Macarius, who had mystical experiences of light and proclaimed that the whole soul had become a spiritual eye and entirely light.[96] Macarius reminds me of a former co-worker in the limo industry who was a self-proclaimed, "Light Worker." He spent many

---

[91] Acts 17:18-28 (NIV).
[92] "The Doctrine of the Virgin Mary and Holy Wisdom," Encyclopedia Britannica, https://www.britannica.com/topic/Christianity.
[93] Holmes, III, *A History of Christian Spirituality*, 30.
[94] Ibid.
[95] See Acts 2:42-47.
[96] Holmes, III, *A History of Christian Spirituality*, 35.

afternoons trying to recruit me into the study of Light Workers. Fortunately, the Holy Spirit advised me against such practice as it would have opened doors to the demonic spiritual world through channeling and other meditative exercises.

*Eastern Mysticism Spirituality*

Interestingly, Dionysius goes beyond the text with his eisegesis of the mystery of God. Indeed, Paul tells us that the mystery of God has been revealed: *Making known to us the mystery of his will, according to his purpose, which he set forth in Christ as a plan for the fullness of time, to unite all things in him, things in heaven and things on earth.*[97] Therefore, the mystery is no longer a mystery; it is the hidden plan of salvation in Christ for both Jew and Gentile. One might contend that it is a stretch to define the mystery as the *luminosity of God,*[98] though light is clearly a part of the divine Logos.

Many of these heretical teachings were fleshed out and condemned at numerous Ecumenical Councils. Some views, several would argue, were not necessarily unorthodox, but rather, differences in opinion as to the spiritual nature of Christianity. However, there were obvious dangers regarding allegory, kataphatic moralism, Alexandrian spirituality, Neo-Platonic thought processes, and paganism.

I believe that God allows us to wrestle with our differences and when an agreement cannot be reached on a particular doctrine or topic, a council of like-minded believers can be convened to democratically resolve the issue. Church councils have actually taken place since the first century in Jerusalem.[99]

*Ancient West Spirituality*

Remarkably, the Western mind tends to be more kataphatic and affective.[100] This makes sense in light of our deep heart connection to spirituality over the more intellectual illumination of the mind. The Western church had traditionally read the Fathers of the East through the filter of Augus-

---

[97] Eph. 1:9-10 (ESV).
[98] Holmes, III, *A History of Christian Spirituality*, 40.
[99] See Acts 15.
[100] Holmes, III, *A History of Christian Spirituality*, 43.

tine.[101] Augustine was interested in encountering a personal God in community. This may be why Martin Luther was drawn to his teachings. Like Augustine, Luther emphasized a communal aspect of Christianity with a keen awareness of God's grace for salvation.

### *Spirituality in the Heroic Age*

Eastern mysticism focused on the receptive heart; whereas, Western mysticism focused on the action of the eyes.[102] We *see* the judgment of God in our hearts and this develops a longing for humility, patience, and repentance. The barbarians focused their spirituality towards objects such as the cross, the real presence in the Eucharist, the Blessed Virgin, and the Scriptures.[103] It's interesting because on the one hand, it infers that our Western Christianity was influenced by barbarian paganism, but on the other hand, it reveals that God can use what man intended for evil for His good (see Gen. 50:20).

### *Spirituality in the High Middle Ages*

Both Anselm and Bernard of Clairvaux were very inspirational to me when I wrote my daily devotional, *Moved by the Spirit*. And, like them, I too struggle between love and intellect.[104] Bernard explains how free will or "free consent" involves humility that leads towards the absence of the compulsion to sin, then to the possibility of choosing not to sin, and finally at death—the inability to sin.[105] If you've been actively working on your relationship with Christ, you are probably somewhere at the end of the compulsion to sin and at the beginning of choosing not to sin.

### *The Spirituality of the Schoolmen*

Hugh of St. Victor searched for deeper meanings behind the biblical narrative. As mentioned before, there is room for allegory in the Bible, but only when the symbolism is backed up by another biblical author, or ex-

---

[101] Ibid.
[102] Ibid., 49.
[103] Ibid., 51.
[104] Ibid., 56.
[105] Ibid.

plained by Jesus, Himself. Hugh gives us a beautiful image of Noah's Ark being built as equated to our human hearts that God is building.[106]

Before Bible college, I was very much into the allegorical and typological interpretation of Scripture, for I belonged to a Charismatic church and that was all that they taught. It's kind of a double-edged sword in a sense. The allegory is what kept me coming back for more; it really got my juices flowing and brought a somewhat magical approach (for lack of better term) to Scripture. On the other hand, if I simply believed every interpretation that any given ministry leader put forth, how would I ever know which one was correct? So, now that I'm learned, I err towards the safe hermeneutical approach that I've been taught in school. But I think that Hugh is relatively safe with using a heart building analogy in relation to Noah's building of the Ark. Indeed, God is building us into His likeness through the power of the Holy Spirit, but perhaps, we'll need His safe passage a bit longer than forty days and forty nights.

The Victorines were medieval men. Unlike the reformers, they believed in a continuity between nature and super-nature, and a progression in faith that results from ascetic discipline. Holmes notes that "Richards's discussion of ecstasy would be much too rich for the blood of a reformer."[107] I believe this is because of the Enlightenment worldview of the Renascence period. No longer were concepts and theories simply evaluated by the reputation of the speaker; now principles and explanations needed to be scientifically proven and administered. This was a drastic paradigm shift in philosophical thinking.

### Byzantine Spirituality

Byzantine spirituality had a few striking facets to it. They emphasized light as a divine energy (ἐνέργεια) as the Logos of God's light synthesized with the light that was in man.[108] Indeed, the contrast between light and darkness can be seen throughout the Bible. This is a reminder that Christians must always be the light in this dark world; illuminating the hope of Jesus Christ to our fellow image-bearers.

---

[106] Ibid., 63.
[107] Ibid., 64.
[108] Ibid., 89.

The Byzantine culture also prayed with their heart as opposed to their mind. With our new identities in Christ, we too must utilize our hearts when we pray to the Father. I try and do this every time I engage with the Holy Spirit.

*Spirituality in the Modern Period*

The modern period of spirituality consisted of the Spanish School, Italian School, French School, the English School, Classical Protestantism, Radical Protestantism, Pietism, and Contemporary Spirituality. The Spanish School followed the spiritual exercises passed down from Ignatius to enhance the degrees of mystical experience.[109] We see some of these exercises still used in contemporary spirituality such as directed prayer, meditation, and growth in intimacy with God.

The Italian School of spirituality is said to be above all, "a religion of love."[110] Love is the greatest gift of all; (see 1 Corinthians 13:13) therefore, along with art, virtual predestination (perhaps, a precursor to Luther's position of single predestination, as opposed to Calvin's view of double-predestination or "formal predestination"), and fighting against the self, the Italian focus was also centered in love.

The French School catered to the likes of Frances de Sales who had a five-step meditation process involving preparation, consideration, affections, conclusion, and spiritual nosegay.[111] The term, "nosegay" or "nose happy" came from a time when people of the period would wear flowers on them to combat the strong stench of the city sewer system. Similarly, Sales' method involved carrying what was meditated upon by the believer throughout their day.

The English School of spirituality utilized a contemplative approach to prayer and meditation.[112] This approach to prayer has been most beneficial to me personally. I often sit for hours contemplating what God is revealing

---

[109] Ibid., 98.
[110] Ibid., 103.
[111] Ibid., 106.
[112] Ibid., 112.

to me during our time together. Sometimes, the answer to my question is *yes*, sometimes it's *no*, and quite often, it's *not yet*.

The mystical poets of the 16th century also contributed greatly to English spirituality.[113] Poetic works from Donne, Herbert, Vaughan, Traherne, and Crashaw often stirred emotion and raised questions about the eschaton. T.S. Eliot was said to have drawn some of his gloomy imagery from Donne and the other Caroline spiritualists.[114]

Of course, German spirituality would not be complete without the influence and passion of Martin Luther. Luther, borrowing much from Augustine, escaped his torment of perpetual sins by developing his doctrine of *Sola Fide*. For Luther, spirituality was much more about enjoying the freedoms of the gospel through Christ's sacrifice on the cross than it was about earning favor through merit.

According to Holmes, Luther was "very much in the German mystical tradition...which is rooted in Dionysian spirituality."[115] It is rather curious that so many of the Western church Fathers draw their spiritual theologies from Dionysius. Dionysius most likely lived in the 5th century, had greater influence in the West than in his native East, was speculative and apophatic, and taught in the same tradition as Evagrius and Gregory of Nyssa.[116] One connection between Dionysius' teachings and the Reformers is that they both focused on mixing Scripture with liturgy.

Radical Protestantism spirituality emphasized that the Holy Spirit speaks directly to the believer. This still holds true today. I've personally heard from the Holy Spirit through prayer and meditation and have recorded what was revealed to me in my mind. The way I discern the Spirit's words from my own, is when it's been backed up by Scripture; when in doubt, it's always good to double-check. The prodigious Jack Hayford agrees:

Many millions often hear the voice of God speaking within their hearts. Sometimes God speaks instructively...sometimes He speaks with

---

[113] Ibid., 114.
[114] Ibid.
[115] Ibid., 124.
[116] Ibid., 39.

inner promptings that come as divinely given intuition, insights or warnings…sometimes He speaks with prophetic words…but *always* He speaks
on the basis that we know, love, study, and search the Scriptures. They are
our source of sufficiency as far as truth and wisdom are concerned. [117]

Lastly, the contemporary spiritual scene includes the spiritual theology
of Weil, Hammarskjold, Thomas Merton, and Martin Luther King.[118] Many
of these contemporaries were influenced by Neo-Platonism, Eastern Mys-
tics, and even Gandhi. The difference today, being that we now recognize
our *nous* or, "mind" as an ontological makeup of community and body.

The contemporary history of spiritual formation can be traced to post-
Vatican II (post-1965) reformers within the Roman Catholic Church, who
sought to find ways to educate and train new priests in a manner that was
appropriate to Vatican II ideals. This formative perspective began to spread
into and was adopted by the Association of Theological Schools, and as an
increasing number of evangelical schools began joining them in the 1970s
and 1980s, the ideals spread throughout the academic and theological strata
of Christianity, particularly in the United States. While initially aimed at academic and pastoral leadership, Houston notes that the Protestant ideal of
the priesthood of all believers pushed churches to expand this formative
ideal to all individuals.[119]

On a popular level, the formation movement emerged, in part, with
the publication of Richard Foster's *Celebration of Discipline* in 1978, which
introduced and popularized a set of spiritual disciplines as historical practices beyond Bible study, prayer, and church attendance that may lead to religious maturity and spiritual growth.[120]

Even though formal spiritual theological education did not arrive until
the mid-twentieth century, theologians in the first millennium wrote theology out of a church conviction versus an academic setting and thus all their

---

[117] Hayford, *Living the Spirit-Formed Life*, 38.
[118] Ibid., 151-153.
[119] Houston, "The History of Spiritual Formation - James Houston and Bruce Hindmarsh:
Open Biola," *Open Biola*, https://cct.biola.edu/the-history-of-spiritual-formation-james-
houston-and-bruce-hindmarsh/.
[120] Ibid.

theology was "spiritual" in a sense. Theologians up to the end of the thirteenth century often wrote and studied on their knees.[121]

*Facets of Spiritual Theology*

There are several facets of spiritual theology that I have discovered during my studies of spiritual formation. Perhaps, the most comprehensive text pertaining to these facets is written by, Simon Chan and titled, *Spiritual Theology: A Systematic Study of the Christian Life*.

Chan mentions that before the enlightenment, spiritual formation was generally regarded as an exercise.[122] I find this to be true, especially in the extant writings of medieval theologians, such as Anselm and Bernard of Clairvaux. These theologians would often practice contemplation and prayer as methods of engagement on a deeper and intimate level with the Holy Spirit.

Universalism was promoted by many mid-century philosophers. A thought-provoking observation by Chan regarding Jurgen Moltmann is that Moltmann took a universalist approach to Pneumatology.[123] Certainly, universalism has been around since the late eighteenth century, if not prior to that period through the philosophies of Origen of Alexandria, yet to assert that all religious belief systems have practitioners who possess the indwelling of the trinitarian God, would be both unorthodox and heretical (see 1 Cor. 6:17, Eph. 4:4). This is a stark reminder that syncretism is still alive and well, even in the West. We must be careful to not fall into the age-old trap of worshiping Christ along with every other god, for our God is a jealous God, indeed.

In recent years, the popular book and later film, *The Shack*, had gained notoriety for its feel-good approach to spirituality in which God forgives even the most egregious evils imaginable, whether the guilty party asks for His forgiveness or not. Yet, would God be a just God if there was no ultimate accountability for our evil deeds? If God is eventually going to grant everyone immunity from their sins, wouldn't that logically include the sin of

---

[121] Dr. Blom, personal correspondence, June 14, 2020.
[122] Chan, *Spiritual Theology*, 16.
[123] Ibid., 27.

denying the divinity of Jesus Christ? What would be the incentive to do good? What fear of consequence would exist? What did Jesus die for? These are all questions we need to ask ourselves before accepting theological positions that have already been labeled heretical by ecumenical church councils.[124] Therefore, we must realize that universalism theology is not dead, and has already made its way into contemporary books and films.

Some Asian liberation theologians use Shamans to discern "the good" for them.[125] Knowing very little about Shamanism, personally, I cannot fully deny or confirm this sentiment. What did strike me regarding Shamanism was one incident in which my wife, Lisa, a native of Mongolia, visited her family back home a few years ago. During her visit, her parents took her to become reacquainted with various family members that she hadn't seen in quite some time. On one such outing, her younger cousin, a self-proclaimed Shaman, declared that our house was full of light and that my wife would benefit greatly by following her husband (*me*) in his journey of Christianity.

The intriguing part of the entire ordeal was that my wife's cousin had never seen or visited our home, and had never met me personally, nor would have known which religion I followed. It made me realize, that even belief systems that are not aligned with Christian faith traditions must ultimately submit to the definitive "good," which is Christ Jesus, Himself.

The nature of the Pentecostal movement can often lead to subjective practices. I found in my own experience with the Charismatic church, that the strong drive for spiritual renewal often oversteps the reality of the working of the Holy Spirit. My personal interactions with miraculous spiritual occurrences have been more sporadic as opposed to forced. Author and professor of Theology at Dallas Theological Seminary, Dr. Jack Deere,

---

[124] Origen and a form of apocatastasis were condemned in 544 by the Ecumenical Patriarch Mennas of Constantinople, and the condemnation was allegedly ratified in 553 by the Fifth Ecumenical Council. Apocatastasis was interpreted by 19th-century Universalists such as Hosea Ballou (1842) to be the same as the beliefs of the Universalist Church of America. However, until the middle of the 6th century, the word had a broader meaning. While it applied to a number of doctrines regarding salvation, it also referred to a return to both a location and an original condition. Thus, the Greek word's application was originally broad and metaphorical. See Hosea Ballou, *The ancient history of universalism: from the time of the apostles* (Charleston: BiblioLife, 2008), 166.

[125] Chan, *Spiritual Theology*, 44.

notes, "James insists miracles are normal—says Elijah was a man just like us (Jas 5.17-18). We humanize the Bible because we've been trained to read it in the light of our experience rather than in terms of the experience of the people actually in it."[126]

One facet to keep in mind when dealing with the sin in our lives is that if one goes through life blaming the world, the flesh, and the devil for their actions, then their moral and spiritual development will be blocked.[127] Too frequently, I stumble upon Christians who blame their past circumstances for their present events and choices. I always tell people that your past does not define you, what you do in terms of advancing your relationship with Christ, and restraining and repenting of sinful behaviors, defines you because God is not ignorant of the condition of our hearts.

There is a fine balance between subjective spirituality and objective spirituality. As mentioned, there are inherent dangers in subjective Christianity when it comes to biblical truths. I've always guarded myself when speaking of my personal Pentecostal or Charismatic spiritual experiences. I do this because if my experience doesn't match objective biblical truths, then I must question my experience. For example, if I hear (in my head) that God is telling me that Jesus will return this year on Passover, this contradicts Matthew 24:36. Therefore, I must re-examine which spirit is telling me this information; perhaps it is not from the Holy Spirit after all.

One interesting facet of spiritual theology is in regard to worship music. Chan argues that most contemporary choruses are shallow in context and/or dubious in theology.[128] My undergraduate theology professor used to complain about this concept quite a bit. He would argue that there is no point in singing along with worship music that promotes poor theology. Similarly, my Old Testament History and Poetry professor used to tell of an old seventy's Christian song called "Hallelu". Unfortunately, the chorus echoes the title, and misses the most vital part of the word, *Jah,* as in *Yahweh.* Professor Hull would complain, "They keep saying, 'hallelu, hallelu, oh my darlin' hallelu,' 'praise the, praise the' instead of 'praise the LORD. Hallelujah!'"

---

[126] Deere, *Surprised by the Voice of God,* 25.
[127] Chan, *Spiritual Theology,* 65.
[128] Ibid., 166.

It is imperative to realize that throughout our spiritual journeys, a spiritual friendship with members of the opposite sex can quite easily degenerate into a sensual one, or what may be regarded as a false friendship. This takes place because the motive is not to bring our friends closer to Christ, but rather, to bring our friends closer to us. I learned this fact the hard way, specifically during my mid-twenties. I failed to see red flags appear as I befriended a woman who was looking for more than just friendship. And, sadly, many times it was I who was looking for more than just friendship. This is why I agree with Francis de Sales' advice to remove myself from the presence of a false friendship,[129] and I find it best to proactively distance myself from people of the opposite sex. Not to say, that one cannot be friends with women or even counsel them spiritually, but it must be done wisely, as Satan surely knows our weaknesses. It is always wise to counsel others in the presence of a spouse, or another church leader of the opposite sex in a public setting.

*Spiritual Formation in the Digital Age*

The impact of technology on spiritual formation may be much more pervasive and significant than we now realize. Navigating through the digital age as a spiritual formationist can be difficult. With a never-ending plethora of gadgets and devices, one can get caught up in the product while forgetting about the Maker. Like all of creation, a Creator is behind the work of art. Apple founder and pioneer, Steve Jobs, once had his staff of technological gurus sign their names onto a sheet of drafting paper that was later engraved onto the motherboards of the revolutionary Macintosh computer when it came out in the early eighties. Some of his staff asked him why he would have them sign something that, unless someone took the computer apart, no one would ever see? His response was, "Real artists sign their work."[130]

Indeed, God has signed His work in the vastness of creation. You can see His signature everywhere you look. Behind every invention that mankind has thought of, is a brilliant designer who dwells in the heavens. In his book, *IGods*, Craig Detweiler notes:

---

129 De Sales, quoted in Simon Chan, *Spiritual Theology*, 177.
130 Isaacson, *Steve Jobs*, 134.

*Technology that heals is a great thing, a God-given gift…God's presence is the power source, the only illumination we will need…ostensibly, our finest achievements in art, music, drama, and literature may make the cut of the glory and honor of the nations. This encourages us to create something beautiful.* [131]

God's hand is guiding the technological age, but who gets the glory when it's all said and done? Certainly not us, I hope. The reality is that technology cannot be eliminated, and it is useful, but it is also dangerous. We tend to celebrate technology as God's gift but often refuse to prostrate ourselves before the gift-giver.

Thankfully, spiritual formation is not dependent upon technology. The earliest practitioners had nothing, but candlelight and God's words written upon their hearts. It wasn't until the Reformation period that the Bible was translated into native tongues and distributed amongst the common people. Before that, people listened to God's words read to them as they reflected and prayed upon their meaning. We still do this today.

Once I was by the river, on my phone with one hand, and with a Bible in the other. One of the passersby said, "You should look up from your phone and enjoy this beautiful nature." I couldn't help but smile because it made me realize that there's more to life than sitting on our phones as God's creation dances before our eyes, often unnoticed by us. Next time I go to the river, I'll be sure and leave my phone in my pocket.

*Conclusion*

Spiritual theology has changed over the ages but remains consistent in its quest to form a more solid relationship with Jesus Christ. Beginning with the Twelve, and ending with us, there has never been a generation of people who have not benefited greatly from spiritual formation.

Spiritual theology is a pragmatic and didactic study of spiritual formation which helps in rediscovering our own goals of relating to Jesus Christ and the Father in more meaningful and intimate ways. As such, we must utilize contemplation more in our actions, and during our prayer time

---

[131] Detweiler, *IGods*, 223-224.

with the Lord. If we spend time seeking God in total self-abnegation, we can touch the depths of our own souls. This is necessary in our journey to move deeper by the power of God into the hiddenness of God.

# CHAPTER 3

## Spiritual Disciplines and How They Apply Today

Spiritual disciplines can be akin to a runner training for the greatest race of his life. When I ran on the track team in high school, many, many years ago, I wasn't sprinting repeatedly to get my 1600-meter time faster. I was running three, four, and five miles, building my endurance so that when I ran the one-mile race in competition, my body was prepared to exceed even my own expectations. I eventually got second place in a track meet with a 5:27 mile time. Oh, how I wish I was still young. Kenneth Boa explains that:

> We desire to know Christ more deeply, but we shun the lifestyle that would make it happen. By relegating the spiritual to certain times and activities, we are ill-prepared to face the temptations and challenges of daily living in a Christlike way. It is easy to deceive ourselves into thinking that without the active and painful formation of godly character, we will have the capacity to make the right choices whenever we need to. But if we have not been exercising and training and practicing behind the scenes, we will not have the skill (wisdom) to perform well when it counts.[132]

We all get inundated with life's responsibilities at times. When I was in college, I was also helping to take care of my wife and three small children,

---

[132] Boa, *Conformed to His Image*, 78.

pastoring a church, teaching, tutoring, and driving town cars and limousines to help pay the bills. On top of all of that, I still had to find time to spend with friends and church members who relied upon my spiritual advice and guidance; I was overwhelmed.

Author and spiritual formation professor, Donald Whitney states that:

> *The world is more complex than ever, and it becomes more so by the nanosecond. As a result, almost everyone eventually feels the need to simplify. For many people, simplifying means nothing more than "doing less." But simplifying is not so much about doing fewer things as it is about doing the right things. This distinction is even more important when it comes to simplifying the spiritual part of life. For even the "ideal" simple spiritual life (whatever that is) will still be a busy one.*[133]

Life can, and does get busy, so my goal with this chapter is to give the reader-spiritual formation practitioner, a better sense of direction when it comes to their spiritual lives. I want to be cognizant of your time and resources when practicing spiritual formation, so I've included some of the traditions, disciplines, and rules of life that have served me best in my efforts to build a better relationship with Christ. Let us begin with the spiritual traditions.

*Spiritual Traditions*

The following is not an exhaustive list of the common spiritual traditions but will give the reader some insights into my personal experience when engaging with several of my favorite ones. I would encourage you to practice spiritual disciplines consistently and with a heart that is open to listening to what the Holy Spirit has to say to you. Remember, it's not a race, it's a marathon, and you must be willing to train hard to achieve a place in your walk with Christ in which you feel closest to Him.

---

[133] Whitney, *Simplify Your Spiritual Life*, 13.

I've kept my examples in the first person singular to give the reader a sense of how one can utilize these traditions in prayer for themselves. I had the pleasure of communing with the Lord as I allowed His words to speak to my heart. What you will read, is the pure influence of the Holy Spirit; expressed innately in my writing.

*The Contemplative Tradition*

The contemplative tradition involves making God our supreme object in life. The contemplative tradition will encompass seasons of dryness and darkness, but when our desire is for God to manifest His presence, our hearts will surely seek His embrace.[134]

In the deeper recesses of my mind, the contemplative self emerges. It is not always easy to recognize due to my flesh attempting to abate it. Nonetheless, this soul-longing thirst for my beautiful God is not so easily quenched. Traveling through time on this earth is only a temporary moment of exhilaration compared to the endless and bountiful love of Jesus Christ who knows no time limit. As I feel the soft breeze of the wind upon my cheeks, I'm reminded that the Spirit is always with me, wherever I go; wherever I have gone.

Sustaining this level of contemplation is not always easy. Though I am slow to admit that my heart should long for God more than it currently does, I never give up fighting off the demons inside that try and tear me away from the Holy One. To know God is to love God. In my quest to find this intimate knowledge, my heart remains guarded. I must continue to work on letting my guard down so that I can let the love of Jesus Christ enter in.

My greatest strength comes, not only from within, but from without as well. The light of Jesus Christ continues to shine into me so that I can use it to illuminate others. I must turn my face to the Lord as I pray diligently with a contemplative heart, focused on Him and only on Him. I must pray

---

[134] Boa, *Conformed to His Image*, 165.

as Jesus prayed, all through the night in some cases; in earnest and in solitude.[135]

Detachment from the world can help me to attach myself to Christ. I have already taken the necessary steps to proactively detach from the unnecessary distractions of the world in which we live. Faith and trust in God must take precedence over any other facets of my life. Life can often become unbalanced. I try and find my balance by reaching out to the One who gave me life in the first place, God Himself.

*The Spirit-Led Tradition*

The Spirit-led tradition includes a goal of living a balanced Spirit-filled life that seeks to unite the mind and the heart instead of setting them in opposition to each other. The past few decades have seen an explosion of worldwide church growth, and some of the fastest-growing churches have been those who have centered their mission on the fullness of the Spirit.[136]

The Spirit is with me at all times. Where the wind blows, He is there also. Guiding me at all times, discerning the Word from evil. Oh, how I long for the presence of the Holy Spirit to continue to step before me as I make important decisions in my life—helping teach me, helping lead me toward Christ Jesus in my walk-through eternity.

The Spirit is willing and strong, but the flesh is weak. You were with me during the hardest times of my life. You prevented me from making rash decisions; You helped rescue me from dire situations. You spoke love and truth into my life when I felt far from your grasp. I thank you for continuing to dwell in me; for continuing to guide my steps.

As the skies darken, your light shines through the fiercest storm. I can feel your presence manifest itself when I pray, when I witness someone's baptism, and when I read your words within the Holy Scriptures. I never

---

[135] *See, Luke 6:12.*
[136] Boa, *Conformed to His Image*, 291.

take for granted the power you have given me to persevere, and to fight the good fight of faith.

I will continue to guard my relationship with you by trusting in your guidance, and by living the Spirit-led life that Jesus Christ Himself, modeled. I will do my best to allow you to walk before me through this world that so often rebels against you. In order to nurture the areas in which I am weak, I will pray earnestly and in solitude until I hear you speak through that inner voice that has spoken to me so many times before.

I thank you for your presence in my life. As the third member of the trinity, I acknowledge that you are equal to both the Father and Son. You are a gift from Christ Himself that dwells inside me at all times, in all places, and during all circumstances.

*The Holiness Tradition*

The Holiness Tradition centers around the formation process from the inside to the outside. Holiness is a new quality of life that's nature is transformational through consecration. The inside-out process of the spiritual life is the gradual outworking of kingdom righteousness as given to us freely through justification by the sacrifice of Jesus Christ.[137] Boa notes:

By inviting Jesus to examine our intentions and priorities, we open ourselves to his good but often painful work of exposing our manipulative and self-seeking strategies, our hardness of heart (often concealed in religious activities), our competitively driven resentments, and our pride.[138]

To live the Holy life is not easy. I have always envisioned a life free of sin, but alas, if that were possible, why did Jesus have to suffer and die for my sins? Utilizing God's word gives me the strength to overcome temptations as they arise. As the Apostle Peter once said, "Love covers a multitude

---

[137] Ibid., 278.
[138] Ibid.

of sins."[139] God viewed King David's holiness, not through the many sins that he committed, but rather, God looked at David's heart. In this sense, I too strive to live a Holy life through the actions of my heart.

I must guard my strengths in the areas of a pure heart and light of the Spirit. By utilizing the Holy Spirit, I can overcome the three enemies of God. By guarding my heart, I can continue to honor God's piousness. I must nurture my weakness in allowing Satan to enter my thoughts. After all, sin begins in the mind and heart before it is ever acted out in the flesh. Jesus was genuinely tempted in all ways yet was able to overcome those temptations. With this hope, I too can overcome temptation by growing in Christlikeness. I hope to build upon my relationship with the Holy God, not by achieving perfectionism, but by resisting the devil so that he will flee from me.

### The Compassion Tradition

The compassion tradition involves relational spirituality. The closer we walk with God, the more we are empowered to manifest our love for Him through acts of love and service to others.[140] Relational Christianity is both vertical and horizontal; meaning that we build our relationship vertically with the Father, Son, and Holy Spirit and at the same time, that dependable relationship develops horizontally in loving our neighbors.

The Triune God is three-in-one. My Lord and Savior is in constant relationship within Himself, and within me. My God is intimately active in my life at every moment; He is interacting with me, guiding me, believing in me. He has always been in relationship with us, and He always will be in relationship with us.

To love God completely is to surrender all things to Him. My identity is found in Jesus Christ. I often see myself as a sinner trying to become a

---

[139] 1 Pt. 4:8 (Emphasis mine).
[140] Boa, *Conformed to His Image*, 42.

saint; God sees me as a saint who sins. With this motivation and encouragement, I am able to share God's love with all those around me.

I have a strong love for mankind. Even if someone has not accepted Christ into their life, I can love them as being made in the image of God. This is a strength in which I can guard by reminding myself that love for others is important to God. So important, in fact, that He couples it with love for Himself in the Great Commandment.

Having compassion for others has helped me greatly in relating to my brothers and sisters in Christ. I need to nurture my quick-witted reaction when under stress or criticism of others. Jesus has great affection and tenderness for us; therefore, I must have that same affection for others. If I remember that I too have sins to overcome, I can better appreciate when others sin against me. No one is righteous in this life, not one. Only through the death and resurrection of Jesus Christ, can we be righteous via our faith, before the Almighty God.

I experience a deep feeling of the Holy Spirit's presence when sharing the gospel message with others, loving others, and having compassion for others. By illuminating God's love from within myself, I also shine my love into others. I emerge victorious when I have a love for one another. In the event that I forget myself and my purpose in this life, I will look toward the cross and remember the love that God had for me on it.

### The Word-Centered Tradition

The Word-centered tradition or "devotional spirituality" is the practice of sacred reading, aka, *Lectio Divina*. It consists of moving from the mind to the heart through reading, meditation, prayer, and contemplation. The ancient monastics approached Scripture much in this way, through personal orientation, meditation, and prayer.[141]

---

[141] Ibid., 175.

In the cool breeze of a spring afternoon, or late at night in the confines of my seclusion, I meditate on the Word both day and night. Such beautiful words written by both, inspired authors, and the Holy Spirit. God's word is timeless. The world will fade away, but God's Word will never fade away. I must guard my strengths in allowing the Holy Spirit to illumine the Word of God for me. I must nurture and work on the areas of pride and intellect so that I stay humble in my knowledge of the Word. Scripture is important in Spiritual battle. Like Jesus, I too can resist temptation by utilizing the Scriptures. The things that Jesus said and did were often rooted in the Old Testament Scriptures.

These traditions are all part of a process of living a spiritually formed life. The five traditions are not in competition with each other, but rather, they complement each other to provide for a well-rounded form of Christianity.

The compassion tradition integrates with the contemplative tradition because it requires discernment through prayer. The Spirit-led tradition integrates with the contemplative tradition through prayer and trust in the Lord to allow the Holy Spirit to guide us in our spiritual journey. The compassion tradition integrates with the Holiness tradition by motivating us to express love in very tangible ways. Lastly, the Word-Centered tradition integrates with all the traditions by accentuating the various elements of each tradition through the very words of God.

Each of these traditions requires the power of the Holy Spirit to enhance and enlighten us as we focus on bettering ourselves for the body of Christ. There are components of each tradition that we will naturally do better in, but we can always take more time in solitude and prayer with the Father so that we can better represent Christlikeness in the areas that need improvement.

### The Incarnational Tradition

Finally, the incarnational tradition concerns itself with the relationship between spirit and matter. In short, God manifests through material means. Richard Foster identifies the incarnational tradition as a sacramental way of living that speaks powerfully to the crying need to experience God as truly manifested and active in our daily lives.[142] In other words, we are to humbly submit to the Father and participate in His will for our lives.

*Help me, Lord, to remember that religion*
*is not to be confined to the church, or closet, nor exercised only in prayer and medita-*
*tion,*
*but that everywhere I am in Thy presence.*
*So may my every word and action have a moral content…*
*May all the happenings of my life prove useful and beneficial to me. May all things*
*instruct me*
*and afford me an opportunity of exercising some virtue*
*and daily learning and growing toward Thy likeness…*
*Amen.*[143]

Jesus Christ modeled all of these spiritual traditions during His incarnational sojourn here on earth. I would encourage you to take the time to become comfortable, confident, and consistent in a few before taking on additional traditional practices. Remember, the Holy Spirit is there with you in this process, ready to hand you the baton once you've built up the endurance to continue in the race.

*Dallas Willard and the Spiritual Disciplines*

I had the pleasure of recently reading *The Spirit of the Disciplines: Understanding How God Changes Lives*, by Dallas Willard. Beginning in chapter two, Willard poses the question: *Where is our practical theology today?* He makes note of the fact that practical theology has not always been successful, and that the church has moved in its theological perspective from period to period in its history.[144] Indeed, this is a dilemma since practical theology involves our efforts of interacting with God to accomplish His divine intent for human existence. So, now we are left with the quandary of maintaining

---

[142] Foster, *Streams of Living Water*, 240.
[143] Kline, *Susanna Wesley*, 42.
[144] Willard, *The Spirit of the Disciplines*, 15.

spiritual discipline while still finding joy in our obedience. Willard addresses this issue five chapters later in which he proclaims:

The practice that prepares us for righteous living includes not only putting your body through the motions of actions directly commanded by our Lord. It also involves engaging in whatever other activities may prepare us to carry out his commands and not just carry them out, but carry them out with strength, effectiveness, and joy. And this is where the standard, well-recognized spiritual disciplines become involved.[145]

This statement couldn't hold truer. Indeed, being completely engaged in one's spiritual actions can only help to strengthen our relationship with the Lord. Often the Lord will inspire me to be involved in activities or events that I wouldn't normally pursue on my own accord. For example, in the past, the Lord has inspired me to participate in groups at Multnomah University such as Book club and Chapel Fellowship. I was also inspired to start a fireside chat group highlighting the many achievements of our professors. In their own unique ways, each of these groups has helped to develop my spiritual disciplines. By engaging Jesus Christ, we first seek Him, and by first seeking Him, we gain His compassion (See Isaiah 55:6-7).

Something we cannot seem to escape from is our sinful thoughts, despite the fact that we are baptized into Christ. Bear in mind, however, that these old impulses are not in themselves sinful because sin has had them in its grip and has twisted them.[146] It is essential that we rebuke the sin from our minds before we sanction it to manifest in someone else's life.

I recently preached a sermon on Colossians chapter three. Willard's assessment of sin relates very well with the doctrine of putting on the new self in Christ. Since we are made new in Christ, our flesh is now able to differentiate between seeing sin as acceptable as opposed to seeing sin as the disgusting thing that it truly is. No longer are we held prisoner to our thoughts and desires but can live free in the light of Jesus Christ.

---

[145] Ibid., 119.
[146] Ibid., 115.

Like I had touched on at the beginning of this chapter, Willard compares training the body and mind in a physical and secular way to training the soul for spiritual activities. He lists a few activities that seem to serve most Christians in their advancement of spiritual discipline. Among these are journaling, rejecting sleep to concentrate on spiritual matters, Sabbath-keeping, physical labor—even common everyday activities like grocery shopping or banking.[147]

*The Spirit of the Disciplines* ends with a didactic look at how the disciplines intertwine with world power structures. Contrary to what you might hear in today's post-modern society, Jesus Christ did not belong to any political party and was very much in opposition to the Roman political government. Jesus once stated that what belongs to Caesar should be given to Caesar, yet what belongs to God should be given to God.[148] Thus, we have our first separation of Church and State. This is one reason that we cannot expect politicians to uphold high Christian standards in the same way devout Christians do. Willard seemingly agrees:

It is too difficult for ordinary people. In fact, it is impossible, as the record of human government shows. Turmoil, insurrection, and revolution are inevitable in and open society where the officials are corrupt. Ultimately, the Saints—and by this we do not mean a political party of "saints"-must be the ones to judge the earth. Only saints of the faith of Abraham and Paul are capable of governing as God (and humans) would have it, because they work in the power of God and have the character to bury it without corruption.[149]

*Disciplinary Rules*

Spiritual disciplinary rule, or "The Rule of Life" as some theologians refer to it, is not a set of rules that make us acceptable before God, that

---

[147] Ibid., 157.
[148] See Mark 12:17.
[149] Willard, *The Spirit of the Disciplines*, 249.

would be legalism. Instead, disciplinary rules are patterns of living our lives in which we aim to achieve proficiency. According to Simon Chan, "Rule enables people to plod along at the 'slow and steady' pace to accomplish far more spiritually than those who rely on unpredictable, sudden spirts of inspiration."[150] If we embrace a particular rule, it helps us to commit to a spiritual pattern of living.

A rule of *life*, must cover the whole of life and spiritualize our entire existence; therefore, a balance between a life orientated rule and a prayer orientated rule is ideal.[151] Some examples of spiritual rules are: cultivating spiritual friendships, family devotions, grace before meals, participation in the life and worship of the church, social involvement in the world, prayers before and after leaving work (more on the power of prayer in chapter six).

Daily devotionals are great tools for giving us a basis in which we can begin our meditation on God's Word, as well as an openness to hear from the Spirit of God. As a disciplinary rule, reading devotionals need not be extensive, in fact, a mere fifteen to twenty minutes per day is a great starting point and will prevent the rule from feeling like a burden. I highly recommend picking up a copy of my devotional, *Moved by the Spirit: A Daily Devotional & Living Doxology* from your favorite Christian retailer. I have several spiritual insights and scriptural verses to meditate upon, and each entry is merely half a page long.

Below is a list of five spiritual exercises to incorporate while engaging with devotionals:

    I.       Preparation

             Ask the Holy Spirit to quiet your mind and remove all distractions.

             Ask God to search your heart and bring to remembrance any known sin.

             Ask the Holy Spirit to illumine your mind as you reverently read Scripture or some other book.

---

[150] Chan, *Spiritual Theology*, 191-192.
[151] Ibid., 194.

II.      Spiritual Reading

Utilize a Bible reading guide that contains systematic readings that cover the entire Bible over a given period.

III.     Meditation

This follows naturally from our spiritual reading. Use a traditional or modern method that suits you. There is no one best method of meditation. The best method is one that you can use effectively.

IV.     Thanksgiving

We must thank God for helping us understand His Word, and beyond that, if we make it a habit to "count our blessings, name them one by one" we will begin to have a very different perspective on the world around us.

V.     Record-Keeping

For many, petitionary and intercessory prayers are haphazard. We promise to pray for someone we meet in church and then forget about it until the following week when we meet again. The only sure way to remember to pray (and keep our promise) is to write it down. Another way is to pray right then and there. Writing down prayer requests is a great way to stay organized as well as spread our petitions evenly through the week.[152]

Whichever spiritual rule we engage in, it's important to stay committed and consistent in our attempt at honoring the Father. All glory goes to God; therefore, we must make the effort to follow disciplinary rules as we participate in godly worship. "So, whether you eat or drink or whatever you do, do it all for the glory of God."[153]

---

[152] An adaptation of, "A Suggested Plan for Set Devotions" by Chan. See Chan, *Spiritual Theology*, 193.
[153] 1 Cor. 10:31 (NIV).

While practicing the disciplines, we must wrestle with both God and the devil in the desert of life, forever climbing Mt. Carmel in our ascent towards perfection in Christ. We need to be willing to fight our demons and be served by God's angels, realizing that at times, we may be unable to discern between the two. This is when the necessity is to place our trust in the Lord above all else, to allow the Holy Spirit to guide our lives in meaningful and obedient ways that both honor and glorify the Father.

It is vital that we read the Scriptures more spiritually and less logically. And, to experience God in a more intimate way, not merely on a propositional level. There is no permanent resting place or formula that captures all of God; perfection lies in the desire for God and desiring to get to know God. This is what we should live for.

By exercising recollection, we remain in the presence of God by turning to Him at regular times throughout the working day. We have an obligation to try to always place ourselves in the reverence of God, for when we are before Him, we are indeed standing on Holy ground.

It is a great idea to acknowledge God more in all of our circumstances and decisions. Sometimes we have an improper attitude of devising our plans for our lives, wanting to be in full control and unwilling to surrender ourselves to God. By trusting in the Lord in all of our circumstances, both present and future, we will honor the fact that He will make our paths straight. I've learned that the more obedient I am to the Lord, the more He rewards me with things that are beneficial to my life and the life of my family. He is a loving God, undeniably.

We can also utilize the Prayer of Examen regularly to engage in better self-examination and reflection. The Prayer of Examen is a way of prayer developed by Saint Ignatius where the explicit goal is to notice what God is doing in our lives. This prayer process is intended to develop in us greater awareness and sensitivity to the wonderful ways God is at work in our world and in our lives.

Another great spiritual exercise is to focus on the Word of God more deeply than before. We must remember to read and meditate, as well as pray both before, and after, we read any of God's holy words. We ought to read spiritually, listening to the Holy Spirit and journaling or jotting down what He reveals to us about God's Word. We can look for how what we are reading pertains to our own lives and how we are a part of the marvelous Christian story. Try to set aside the academic analysis of the Scriptures and refocus on contemplation and meditation of them instead.

Lastly, continue to read and write devotions to the Lord as you engage in quiet time with Him in your rule of life. I first prepare my mind and spirit by removing all distractions, then participate in spiritual reading, followed by meditation, thanksgiving, and then petitionary prayer. We may need to adjust our personal rule, depending on if we want it to be more life orientated or prayer orientated, but a nice balance between the two is never a bad thing.

*Spiritual Direction*

Thus far, we've looked at spiritual formation concerning our own betterment in moving towards spiritual perfection in Christ. The subsequent section pertains to what is known as spiritual direction. Spiritual direction, simply put, is guiding people in making wise choices so that they might grow in spiritual maturity.[154] Therefore, spiritual formation involves an experiential awareness of God's presence that leads to conversation, communion, and ultimately authentic transformation of the entire person by an internal yielding to God's will; whereas, spiritual direction is the practice of guiding others in that process.

A fully developed disciple of Christ should exhibit several characteristics including fully trusting God, self-discovery, setting boundaries, building a relationship with God, and unity, so that molding one's self into the likeness of Christ is possible. I want us to look at some pragmatic ways in which any spiritual director can assist the directed in becoming perfected in Christ, as well as make sound spiritual decisions independently.

---

[154] Benner & Moon, *Spiritual Direction and the Care of Souls*, 12.

Before anyone can begin spiritual direction, there is one word that will stand in their way; *trust*. Trust is a four-letter word, yet not one that we should be afraid of saying. Long before I ever stepped out of my comfort zone into giving people spiritual advice, I had to decide to trust that God would direct my steps. Indeed, there were times when the journey ahead was full of choppy water and crashing waves, yet as I kept my gaze on Jesus Christ, I learned that it was okay to step out of the boat. Much too often, we attempt to please God instead of simply trusting Him.

John Lynch, Bruce McNicol, and Bill Thrall construct this dichotomy in their book, *The Cure*. These authors paint a vivid image of an intersection in our lives where we can decide to take the path of trusting God or pleasing God.[155] As we inevitably pursue pleasing God, we realize that our self-efforts are merely masked in good intentions.

The real struggle involves resetting our minds to trusting the Lord at all times and in every situation. Several times throughout our lives, we feel frustration and despair when trying to please God by not sinning only to discover that we are in bondage to sin and cannot free ourselves. This is where Christ comes in. It isn't up to us to remove the eternal consequences of sin from our lives. Jesus Christ did that already at the Cross. This, of course, is not an excuse to continue to sin, but rather a sense of freedom from the pain and suffering that sin places upon us. The Apostle Paul explains our righteousness in his letter to the Romans: "This righteousness is given through faith in Jesus Christ to all who believe. There is no difference between Jew and Gentile."[156]

Quite understandably, we tend to shield our sin by wearing masks that disguise who we truly are inside; however, it is important to take our masks off once and a while and enjoy the fresh air of acclimation. Lynch states:

When I discover I'm still hiding, that probably should be the hint that whatever I've tried to cover my shame with, hasn't taken. It wasn't until

---

[155] Lynch, McNicol, and Thrall, *The Cure*, 19.
[156] Rom. 3:22 (NIV).

they [Adam and Eve] trusted, that God did something, providing His own covering for them so that they could be free from hiding and condemnation. [157]

The tussle behind the mask is real. One cannot simply destroy their masks without effort, but the journey of trusting God is not one that we travel alone, it is one in which Christ takes on the burden for us. When we look back at the footprints in the sand and discover only one set, we must realize that it was then that Christ carried us. Trusting in God will ultimately lead to pleasing Him.

Self-discovery plays an intricate role in our relationship with Christ and is an experience we can share with those we mentor. Many times, throughout my life, I've enjoyed walking along the Truckee River near downtown Reno. These are times when I can reflect on life, ponder my goals in this world, think about my children and wife, and most importantly, spend time with Jesus Christ in solitude. There is much power in the ability to spend time with God alone. Jesus set the example for us when He so often would go into the mountains to pray.

Discovering oneself involves two-way communication between us and our creator. Too often our lives are so busy that we do not take the time to stop and listen to what the Lord is trying to tell us. Some of my best sermons were written in the quietness of my home office in which the dawn had yet to break. This is because I *made* time for God to speak to me, regardless of the hour.

Life is full of trials and tribulations. The manner in which we handle these difficult times reveals the true character that lies within each of us. Often times in the face of a devastating situation, we react in an ungodly manner; however, God's Spirit still dwells within us, so it is important to realize that no matter what the enemy brings to the table, we are not alone in facing him.

---

[157] Lynch, McNicol, and Thrall, *The Cure*, 30.

Knowing ourselves is very important, as is knowing where we are at in our journey of faith. David Benner notes that "knowing ourselves must begin by knowing the self that is known by God. If God does not know us, we do not exist."[158] God loves each one of us very deeply. This is because God's love is divine and unconditional. Why then do we continue to sin? Because we are still living in a broken world and sanctification is a lifelong process. The Apostle Paul famously said, "For I do not understand my own actions. For I do not do what I want, but I do the very thing I hate."[159] Our human nature wants us to rebel against God, yet the Holy Spirit that dwells inside of us aims to create perfection in The Holy One.

There are some Christians who base their identity on being a sinner; however, this is not the way that God identifies us. God's love is still directed towards us. Really knowing ourselves can only happen once we realize that we are deeply loved. Benner proclaims:

Sin is more basic than what we do. Sin is who we are. In this regard, we could say that sin is fundamentally a matter of ontology, not simply morality. To be human is to be a sinner. It is to be broken, damaged goods that carry within our deepest self a fundamental fatal flaw—a flaw that masks our original creation goodness and infects our very being. [160]

Setting boundaries also aids in our Christian development as we help others in their journey towards Christ. In his chapter on making the theology of the disciplines practical, Dallas Willard points out that in our hearts we believe that we should be Christlike, however, hardly any of us see this as a real possibility.[161] If suddenly one morning we professed that, "Today I am going to stop sinning," many would look at us as though we were crazy or had some ulterior motive for trying to be less sinful than our Christian brothers and sisters. Yet, on the other hand, if we stated that we do not intend on discontinuing our lives of sin, one may actually question our sal-

---

[158] Benner & Moon, *Spiritual Direction and the Care of Souls*, 45.
[159] Rom. 7:15 (ESV).
[160] Benner & Moon, *Spiritual Direction and the Care of Souls*, 60.
[161] Willard, *The Spirit of the Disciplines*, 12.

vation. By setting boundaries that we refuse to cross, we can make an attempt at removing the sinful desires in a particular area of our lives.

We must advise others of particular patterns that precipitate sinful behaviors. I've discovered that certain "triggers" affect how my mind will react in various situations. For example, if I have been driving a limousine full of beautiful young women during a bachelorette party in the late hours of the evening and my wife and I had just finished arguing about finances before the trip, the trigger would be Satan planting a thought in my mind to try and justify my sexual feelings towards women other than my wife. So, to combat these feelings, I must reset my mind towards God and what would please Him, rather than what momentarily pleases myself.

The paradox with sin is that Satan cannot continue to tempt you in a specific sin if every time he does, you turn and run towards God. This is what is known as repentance. Willard also reports that practicing prayer, fasting, meditation, simple living, and submission to a spiritual overseer are all ways in which we can set boundaries for ourselves that will help us to breathe new life into old disciplines.[162] True character transformation be-

| Relationship | Agenda | Process | Role of the Helper | Freequency of Meeting | Goal of the Learner |
|---|---|---|---|---|---|
| Pastoral Counseling | Set by the counselee | Problem solving, crisis management, healing of past wounds and/or relational issues | Facilitator | Once, on an on-going basis, or when needed | To be "healthy" |
| Discipleship | Set by the discipler | Instruction | Transmitter | Ongoing relationship | Learning incorporation, to become like the teacher/discipler |
| Mentoring | Chosen by mentor and mentee, and influenced by an external such as a workplace or educational institution | Development | Coach | Once, or ongoing relationship | Improvement and growth, to become like or meet the expectations of the external influence |
| Spiritual Direction | Revealed by the Holy Spirit | Noticing, paying attention, praying | Pray-er, listener | Monthly | Imago dei, to become more like Christ, to notice God's presence |

---

[162] Ibid., 25.

gins in the pure grace of God, yet action on the part of the transformed is required in making the Christian a truly different kind of person.

It is essential when setting our boundaries to distinguish pastoral counseling from spiritual direction. Author, Jeannette Bakke, provides a beneficial chart that delineates the roles of pastoral counseling, discipleship, mentoring, and spiritual direction.

Pastoral counseling is in place to stop the hemorrhaging of sin in the Christian's life. While pastoral counseling has great techniques to help the believer cope with their decisions, spiritual direction involves much more qualitative functions. Moon & Benner list several guidelines in which spiritual direction should be applied and practiced, such as: recognizing if helping relationship in direction goes beyond crises, realizing that attention to the operation of grace is central to spiritual direction, knowing that spiritual direction requires a shared confessional stance, that faith in God is central in the spiritual direction process, and issues of surrender and conversion are overt in spiritual direction.[163]

Remember to emphasize the realization that developing oneself into the likeness of Christ must include relationship building between the Christian and God. This is why our prayer lives are so important. Our goal as spiritual directors should be to build others up in a way that is glorifying to God. There is a stark difference between Christian psychology and pastoral care. Psychologists would say, "I'm going to try and help you line up with yourself". Pastors, however, would say, "I'm going to try and help you line up with God." The *care* is what we do to bring people to Christ, but the *cure* is them getting perfected in Christ, whether it is accomplished with our help, or by God Himself. In the book, *The Kingdom Life*, by Alan Andrews, there is an expansion upon this transformational process as reflected upon by spiritual formation scholar, Keith Matthews:

Discipleship to Jesus Christ is a transformational process that begins with regenerated life as a person becomes Jesus' disciple...Transformation

---

[163] Benner & Moon, *Spiritual Direction and the Care of Souls*, 211-213.

continues as the disciple intentionally pursues being conformed to Jesus' image, which is carried out in our everyday world of personal, public, community, and family life.[164]

Matthews further advances his theory by explaining that we must engage in a well-directed effort if we are to grow.[165] This is essential to spiritual growth because without making the effort on the part of the directed, one remains susceptible to sinful practices. We must remember that we become one with Christ at our conversion; therefore, our spiritual growth entails experientially growing into who we already are.

Many Protestant models of spiritual direction are all in agreement that glorification with Christ is the ultimate goal.[166] This type of relationship involves a focus towards God so that when there is a crisis, we will be able to handle it differently than if we didn't have a crisis in the first place. This reaction takes place as we become further conformed to His image.

When I was younger, I used to constantly worry about where my next paycheck would come from and whether or not it would be enough to cover my needs. As I matured in Christ, I realized that the money I earn is ultimately borrowed from God because God provides me with the job to earn the money in the first place. This really took the pressure off of me and placed it on the cross. Jesus already died for my anxiety, so there's no need to worry.
God will provide; He always does.

One could argue that another goal of spiritual direction is to have the directed become independent in his or her choices and spiritual decisions. It will not do much good if every time there is a spiritual crisis situation, the person in crisis has to depend on their spiritual mentor or pastor for the answers. There may be times when the pastors themselves will not have all of the answers, or they are simply not available. This is why it is so vital that

---

[164] Matthews, *The Transformational Process*, quoted in Andrews, *The Kingdom Life*, 85.
[165] Ibid.
[166] Chan, *Spiritual Theology*, 18.

every Christian work towards independent decision making as they seek to be perfected in Christ.

The orthopraxy of spiritual direction involves leading by example yet realizing that we all have doubts sometimes. How does one handle it when there is a lack of faith? What if we have a spiritual breakdown and need mentors of our own to encourage us? We must realize that we might fail more than we succeed, but God is always with us in that process. As we mature in our spiritual journey, God is refining us to His image. Proverbs 25 says:

*As the heavens are high and the earth is deep, so the hearts of kings are unsearchable. Remove the dross from the silver and a silversmith can produce a vessel; remove wicked officials from the king's presence, and his throne will be established through righteousness.*[167]

The Lord is actually removing this cross from us as we go throughout our lives backsliding in sin.

We have just looked at several ways in which we can help our fellow Christians become fully developed disciples of Christ. Trusting God, self-discovery, setting boundaries, building a relationship with God, and unity are all critical in a believer's spiritual formation that ultimately leads to perfection in Christ. The Spiritual director can assist with this process in several ways. Simply listening in a loving way or showing the directed that we have been there before and have overcome our spiritual hurdles can be very powerful.

We should act as their mentor, model, coach, advocate, sponsor, and mediator in an effort to see the directed self-engaged in prayer and fasting or refrain from sexual expression outside of marriage. Letting the directed realize that we are more than their *director*, we are their spiritual *friend.* Recognizing the fruit of the Spirit; love, joy, peace, patience, kindness, etc. are all ways in which spiritual maturity can be measured.

---

[167] Prov. 25:3-5 (NIV).

It is important to realize that our job as spiritual directors is not to cure people but to guide them. Only God alone can cure them if they willingly participate. We must be aware of the differences between psychological care, pastoral counseling, and spiritual direction. In some cases, the directed must be referred out to a specialist in mental health if it is beyond our scope of care.

*Fasting*

Most scholars would agree that an area that is fundamental to strengthening one's spiritual walk, is fasting. Sitting on my bookshelf at home is a book, *Fasting*, by John Eckhart. Eckhart does a fantastic job of juxtaposing fasting practices with Scripture. Early on, Eckhart states:

Fasting is beneficial whether you fast partially or fully. One-day fasts on a consistent basis will strengthen your spirit over time and give you the ability to disciple yourself for longer fasts. Three-day fasts with just water are a powerful way to see breakthroughs…Fasts longer than three days should be done by people with more experience in fasting.[168]

We should consider approaching fasting with humility and sincerity. Don't be like the Pharisees of Jesus' day, who preferred to let everyone know they were physically malnourished (see Matthew 6:16). God rewards what we do in secret, so I would recommend not telling anyone you are fasting and see how God blesses you.

When fasting, be sure and include a prayer with your regiment. It seems obvious, but many people refrain from eating food, yet do not replace the physical nourishment with spiritual sustenance. Remember, fasting is intended to deprive yourself of life's temporary pleasures so that you can indulge in the endless pleasure of Jesus' presence.

If I'm honest with myself, there are many things that I place in front of my time with God. Work, school, watching television, sleeping, thinking

---

[168] Eckhardt, *Fasting*, 4.

inappropriate thoughts, recording music, reading, writing this book, eating too much, and the list goes on and on. If gluttony isn't your weakness, find something else that is and eliminate that desire for a day or so and replace it with prayer and worship. If you run out of things to pray about, recite the Psalms out loud, Surely God will be glad that you took the time to think about Him.

Many high church traditions celebrate the season of Lent. Lent is a season of forty days, not counting Sundays, which begins on Ash Wednesday and ends on Holy Saturday. Lent comes from the Anglo-Saxon word *lencten*, which means "spring." The forty days represent the time Jesus spent in the wilderness, enduring the temptation of Satan and preparing to begin his ministry. Lent is a time of repentance, fasting, and preparation for the coming of Easter. It is a time of self-examination and reflection. In the early church, Lent was a time to prepare new converts for baptism. Today, Christians focus on their relationship with God, often choosing to give up something or to volunteer and give of themselves for others.[169]

Isn't it fascinating that many Catholic Priests will fast for several days before preparing for spiritual battle with the enemy? I've watched several exorcism documentaries in which a Priest will deprive himself of food for more than a week before engaging in a spiritual battle.

Fasting takes time to build up to, but it has so many physical and spiritual benefits. Start off slowly and in an area of your life that you know you can live without. Then, try and build up your spiritual strength to extend your fasting time. I would highly recommend engaging in fasting to heighten your experience and relationship with Christ.

*Conclusion*

---

[169] "What is Lent and Why Does it Last Forty Days?" Ask the UMC, accessed April 21, 2020, https://www.umc.org/en/content/ask-the-umc-what-is-lent-and-why-does-it-last-forty-days.

In this chapter, we looked at several spiritual traditions that help to comprise the spiritual disciplines. We made note of some of the rewards and challenges involving the spiritual disciplines, as communicated in Dallas Willard's book, *Spirit of the Disciplines*. We covered disciplinary rules, spiritual direction, and ended with the power of fasting in the Christian life, both intermittently, and during the season of Lent. I pray that this chapter has given you some valuable insights into what spiritual disciplines are, as well as, some practical examples of how to exercise them for yourself.

# CHAPTER 4

## Spiritual Warfare

Spiritual warfare has been extant since the beginning of time, and perhaps even before that if you consider that the sons of men (angels) witnessed the creation of the earth. According to Scripture, Satan's fall happened sometime prior to the creation of mankind.[170]

The first chapter of Genesis verifies that God's original creation was good, yet Satan is undeniably evil. Therefore, the natural inference is that, like human beings, Satan was created good but fell from that original state.[171] Additionally, the Apostle Paul tells us in 1 Timothy, "He must not be a recent convert, or he may become conceited and fall under the same judgment as the devil."[172] This text indicates that the devil had done something deserving of punishment by exercising his free-will in opposition to the Holy God and Father.

---

[170] See Job 38:4,7. Some biblical scholars reference Ezekiel 28 as alluding to Satan's fall, yet many theologians argue that this is simply referencing an oracle of the King of Tyre and his fallen state; however, God might be revealing a deeper message here. The King of Tyre never lived in the garden of Eden, and certainly the King of Tyre was never created; he was born like the rest of mankind, and finally he was never anointed guardian cherub, which by definition, a cherub is a created being who guards things. The first reference to a cherub is in Genesis where one is placed to guard the entrance to the Garden of Eden after the fall (see Gen. 3:24). See also, Christopher Morgan & Robert Peterson, *Fallen: A Theology of Sin.* (Wheaton: Crossway, 2013), 220.
[171] Morgan & Peterson, *Fallen*, 220.
[172] 1 Tim. 3:6 (NIV).

Fighting Satan is time consuming, painful, and exhausting—so why do it? The answer is that we have no choice. We are, in fact, living in a spiritual war-zone. Whether or not we cognitively recognize this war, we are in it, and being passive will not leave us safe. In fact, doing nothing will lead to spiritual ruin.[173]

You might recall reading in Genesis chapter three when Adam and Eve sinned against God. What did Adam do? He hid from God, or you could say, he *separated* himself from his creator. When we sin, we separate ourselves from the Father. If we continue living in our sins, God may very well give us over to them and we will be forever, eternally separated from the Father.[174]

Many Christians are not aware of the intense psychological trauma that takes place during spiritual battle until the battle is lost. Often, we only notice the outcome or results of demonic attacks, but we do not realize that the smaller attacks of the enemy are building upon each other to reach a culmination of demonic strongholds. A foothold of sinful behavior is only a step away from a stronghold of sinful oppression.

C.S. Lewis, in his chilling book, *The Screwtape Letters*, reveals Satan's phycological warfare tactics:

> *My dear Wormwood, Yes. A period of sexual temptation is an excellent time for working in a subordinate attack on the patient's peevishness. It may even be the main attack, as long as he thinks it the subordinate one. But here, as in everything else, the way must be prepared for your moral assault by darkening his intellect. Men are not angered by mere misfortune but by misfortune conceived as injury. And the sense of injury depends on the feeling that a legitimate claim has been denied. The more claims on life, therefore, that your patient can be induced to make, the more often he will feel injured, and, as a result, ill-tempered.[175]*

Satan, indeed, damages our minds, long before he damages our bodies.

Prayer is a strong weapon against Satan's attacks. As I highlight in the next chapter, prayer must be done powerfully and specifically. Author, Chip

---

[173] Dr. Blom, personal communication, June 30, 2020.
[174] See Rom. 1:22-24.
[175] Lewis, *The Screwtape Letters*, 111.

Ingram, infers that we should pray like we're in a battle with the enemy.[176] We must be honest with ourselves when battling the enemy. If we know the truth, yet we're not following it, then we're being deceived and not wearing the breastplate of righteousness.

The old adversary can arrange his diabolical deeds in such a way that we may experience feelings of being too tired to pray or read the Bible. It's then that Satan starts to say, "You're not worthy to be a pastor, ministry leader, etc."[177] You see, Satan is making us feel guilt intentionally to carry our minds into a dark place, of which, he is more than happy to occupy.

Speaking of psychological spiritual battles, have you ever been so scared that you felt paralyzed? When I was a child, maybe eleven or twelve years old, I had that type of feeling when I was at my grandmother's house once. Indeed, Satan was on the offensive, trying to oppress my thoughts and restrict my movements. I imagine that must be what Hell is like; constant fear and anguish, all done in the absence of God's presence.

*Spiritual Armor*

Any responsible human being will take measures to protect themselves when venturing out into a world of unknown dangers. A motorcyclist wears a helmet in case an unforeseen accident causes him to plummet towards the hardened asphalt below. A football player wears shoulder pads, knee pads, a helmet, and other protective gear knowing that an opponent is often running straight towards him to tackle him onto the ground. The gardener wears protective glasses to shield his eyes from the possible projectiles that might kick up from the bottom of a lawnmower or edger.

All of these items are worn to protect oneself from possible bodily harm. Similarly, we are afflicted by the spiritual weapons of the enemy and need to wear protective armor to prevent injury that could very well lead to death; both spiritual death and physical death. Therefore, we must rely upon the Holy Spirit to structure our prayers and to facilitate putting on the full armor of God.[178] Paul's epistle to the Ephesians gives an excellent metaphorical example of the armor needed to successfully defend ourselves against our adversary.

---

[176] Ingram, *The Invisible War*, 42.
[177] Ibid., 68.
[178] See Eph. 6:18.

*The Belt of Truth*

When I was perhaps twelve or thirteen years old, I remember loose-fitting clothes being in style. It seemed like everyone around me had some type of long dress shirt or oversized sweatshirt. Of course, this was 1989 on the West Coast, but I imagine this style was mirrored from famous 80s Hollywood teen actors. Eventually, belts started to come back into style and long shirts worn by men were being tucked in again.

A Roman soldier, in the wintertime, in the first century, also struggled with long clothing that needed to be tucked in to allow him to move about freely without being obstructed by a dangling robe outside of his belt. This is where the Apostle Paul's term of "girding up his loins" comes from. When a soldier was off duty, he would leave his belt unbuckled, yet when on duty and it was time for battle, his robe was tucked into his belt and his sword would hang from his belt with the shield attached.[179]

The application to us is this: putting on the belt of truth is part of our job as soldiers for Christ. We have the belt of truth and honesty to defend us from the enemy's first form of attack; his lies. In fact, Satan is said to be the father of lies (see John 8:44), and every temptation is predicated on a lie. Lies are unlimited in scope, while the truth is narrow. A key is knowing the Holy Spirit who can expose all lies.

In the Garden of Eden, the first lie that Satan told was, "You will not certainly die."[180] Of course, Adam and Eve most certainly *did* die, and so do the rest of us. Since Satan cannot maintain his lie about the absence of physical death, he's switched his strategy to the absence of spiritual death; trying to convince us that there was no Messiah named Jesus Christ who paid the price for our sins and that there is no hope for a heavenly eternity with our Father; perhaps that's his most damaging lie of all. Don't fall for his lies again; keep fastened your belt of truth.

*The Breastplate of Righteousness*

As Paul wrote his letter to the Ephesians, he wrote it (along with the

---

[179] Ingram, *The Invisible War*, 93.
[180] Gen. 3:4 (NIV).

inspiration of the Holy Spirit) in a very organized and congruent manner. The soldier's breastplate was made of bronze, covered the midsection, and protected the heart; a vital organ that keeps us alive. After we have girded ourselves up in the belt of truth, isn't it quite fitting that we should protect our hearts with righteousness? Since our righteousness is not actually ours, (it is imputed upon us by Christ) we must have the truth of Christ first, for it is fundamental in our battle against the enemy.[181] Imputed righteousness makes experiential righteousness possible.

It is significant to remember that God always judges us by our hearts. We must protect our hearts at all times from demonic attack. Remember the jealousy of King Saul and how it raged against David? Saul was not protecting his heart with the breastplate of righteousness. After God's Spirit had encountered the true heart in Saul, a tormenting spirit was sent to replace it. Today, one might open up this type of demonic activity through Ouija boards or other forms of witchcraft. Be very careful, for where your treasure is, there will be your heart also.[182]

*Feet of Readiness*

About two years ago, my wife bought me a new pair of dress shoes with an intricate rubber pattern designed within the sole. Perhaps, the shoes I had worn for the past five years had seen better days because the bottom sole was smooth and shiny from the various elements that they had been exposed to in the harsh Lake Tahoe environment. My new dress shoes grip really well in the snow.

A Roman soldier's sandals were a first-century version of our modern-day cleats. Alexander the Great is said to have championed, and perhaps even invented them.[183] The Greek army was insured an impressive victory via their sure footing during battle. This is what Paul was picturing for us; a soldier's feet solidly planted in certainty.[184] Ingram notes:

> *Imagine putting on the belt of truth to guard against Satan's deceptions and the breastplate of righteousness to guard against his condemnation. Your vital organs are protected. But what good will that do you if you can't keep your foot-*

---

[181] Ingram, *The Invisible War*, 102-103.
[182] Matt. 6:21 (Emphasis mine).
[183] Ingram, *The Invisible War*, 112.
[184] Ibid., 113.

*ing? You have to be able to support all of your equipment with the kind of foundation that will allow you to keep your backside off the ground.* [185]

In conjunction with his lies about our lack of eternal security, Satan uses false gospels to try and convince us that Jesus is not the way to the Father; that there is another way to salvation. We must stand firm in the Christian faith as it is revealed to us in the Bible. Jesus Christ died for us as sinners and this was the propitiation that satisfied the Father; through our faith in Jesus Christ, we enter into God's kingdom. There is no other gospel.

*The Shield of Faith*

Chip Ingram gives additional insights to some of Paul's language as it pertained to a Roman soldier in the first century when explaining the historical details of the shield of faith:

At the time Paul wrote to the Ephesians, there were two kinds of shields. One was a small, round, handheld shield like the kind you always see in movies about ancient gladiators. That's not what Paul was referring to. The shield in this passage was about four feet high and two and a half feet wide. It had hooks on the sides to link it to other shields in a line so that the entire row of soldiers could advance without exposing themselves to incoming arrows. [186]

The enemy would commonly dip their arrows in pitch, light them, and then fire thousands of them towards the Roman soldiers. In response, the shield used by the Romans was made of two pieces of wood and iron that were spaced apart and wrapped in linen, this way once the flaming arrow penetrated the first shield, there was a gap that would quickly extinguish the flame before it reached the inner shield.[187] This ability to quench the enemy's fiery arrows was the metaphor that Paul used when he spoke of the shield of faith in Ephesians 6:16, and Paul's readers would have known exactly what Paul was talking about.

This faith which has absolute confidence in God recognizes Jesus' victory over sin which enables our shields to quench the oncoming arrows of

---

[185] Ibid.
[186] Ibid., 138.
[187] Ibid., 139.

the enemy. Blasphemous thoughts, hateful thoughts, doubts, and overwhelming times of depression are all lies of fiery darts fired at us by the enemy.[188] This is why we must always have our shield of faith in place, right out in front of us to extinguish even Satan's most sweltering blows.

### The Helmet of Salvation

I played many sports in high school—swimming, track team, and football being the prominent ones. I always appreciated the fact that I had on a helmet, especially in my position as a wide receiver. Several times, I was tackled to the ground only to arise with dirt and grass wedged into the side of my helmet. Imagine what my face would have looked like if I didn't wear one.

There's an allusion in this metaphor to the security we have in our salvation. Ingram says that "It's the certainty of deliverance from sin and the protection of our minds in battle. The helmet of salvation may be seen as the ability to reason logically and wisely from a biblical worldview, no matter how that worldview comes under attack."[189]

Salvation has three tenses in the New Testament: past, present, and future. We *were* saved from the eternal consequences of sin at the cross through justification (see Rom. 8:24) we *are* being saved through sanctification (see 1 Cor. 1:18), and we *will be* saved from the sins of the earth when Christ returns (see 1 Pet. 1:5). The tense that Paul is referring to here is the present. We are constantly being influenced by the world, the flesh, and the devil. Don't believe me? Just think of the last time that you sinned…In your mind. Not long ago, was it? The helmet of salvation must be worn at all times; as soon as we take it off, Satan is free to attack our heads.

### The Sword of the Spirit

Paul finishes up his list of metaphorical Roman armor with the only *offensive* weapon we have in our fight against the enemy; the Sword of the Spirit. The Sword of the Spirit is, indeed, God's Word. A Roman soldier would typically carry a two-foot weapon used in close, hand-to-hand combat. This sword was the only weapon that could be used when the enemy

---

[188] Ibid., 140-141.
[189] Ibid., 149.

was close, and their very lives were dependent upon this weapon. Paul defines the Christian's sword for us in Ephesians 6:17: It *is* the Word of God.[190] Somewhat, a play on words (pun intended), the "Word of God" is commonly referred to as Jesus Christ, Himself,[191] so not only are we using the literary words of God in our attempt to offensively combat our enemy, but we are using Jesus Christ, Himself as a weapon against our adversary.

*Sanctification*

> *Now may the God of peace himself sanctify you completely and may your whole spirit and soul and body be kept blameless at the coming of our Lord Jesus Christ.* [192]

I touched on sanctification a tad in chapter one; however, I'd like to expand upon my thoughts about progressive sanctification a bit more, especially as it pertains to helping us in our ongoing battle against the enemy. If we're not actively fighting against the world, the flesh, and the devil, we're participating with them. Author and Spiritual Formation Professor, Mark Bubeck, highlights something that I've been saying for years, which is that sanctification is a lifelong process.[193] We cannot expect to be fully Christlike at our conversion. When it comes to the spirit regenerating, it's instantaneous, but when it comes to sanctification, it takes time to mirror Christlikeness. Through Spiritual disciplines and time well-spent with the Father, we can move towards perfection in Christ.

One way in which we can move forward in our relationship with God and away from our relationship with the world is through a process that the Holy Spirit is very much involved with, called *progressive sanctification*. Sanctification comes from a Latin word that is a translation of the Greek verb ἁγιάζω, meaning to consecrate, make holy, set apart, purify, etc.[194] It has the same root as the adjective ἅγιος, which means "Holy."

There are primarily three stages of sanctification. Sanctification has a definite beginning at regeneration (when we're born again). A moral change

---

[190] Eph. 6:17 (Emphasis mine).
[191] See John 1:1.
[192] 1 Thess. 5:23 (ESV).
[193] Bubeck, *The Adversary*, 133.
[194] BDAG, *A Greek-English Lexicon of the New Testament and Other Early Christian Literature*, 105.

occurs in our lives at the point of regeneration. Paul talks about the "washing of regeneration and renewal in the Holy Spirit (see Titus 3:5). Once we have been born again, we cannot continue to sin as a habit or pattern of life (see 1 John 3:9).[195] In other words, we still sin, but we are kept from yielding to a life of sin.

I, along with the Bible, argue that sanctification increases throughout life. Progressive sanctification involves our active participation in conjunction with the work of the Holy Spirit. Even though the New Testament speaks about a definite beginning to sanctification, it also sees it as a process that continues throughout our Christian lives. Paul recognized that even though we have been set free from our sins (the eternal consequences of them), sin remains in our lives (see Rom. 6:12-13).

Some theologians take Paul's words in 1 Cor. 6:11 to mean that when you are baptized you are justified as well as fully sanctified.[196] Paul says this in the aorist (Greek past tense, but not a once and for all time action concerning aspect) form, "You 'were' washed; you 'were' sanctified." This means that he's looking back on a completed event, as if he's saying "after Jesus returns, you will have been fully sanctified, *already* justified, fully washed", etc.[197] The author of Hebrews tells us, "Strive for the holiness without which no one will see the Lord."[198]

Sanctification will be completed at death (for our souls) and when the Lord returns (for our bodies). Because there is sin that remains in our hearts, even after salvation, our sanctification can never be completed in

---

[195] Grudem, *Systematic Theology*, 747-751.
[196] How can the Corinthian Christians be at the same time sinners and washed, sanctified and justified? Is Martin Luther's famous statement true, *simul justus et peccator* ("at the same time justified and sinner")? Yes, but this is not the whole picture. Believers are also *washed* and *sanctified*. Sin in the believer's life is incompatible with this new reality in Christ; there is to be a progressive realization of sanctification in our actual experience. This is elsewhere described as the fruits of righteousness (Rom. 6:22; Jas. 3:17–18) or the fruit of the Holy Spirit (Gal. 5:22–23). While Paul is realistic and knows that sin is present among the Corinthian Christians, he is also insistent that the presence of repeated acts of sin which form the character of a person into a fornicator, or a swindler or homosexual or thief, is incompatible with the kingdom of God. Those who become such evildoers through repeated offenses, even though professing Christian faith, will not share in the kingdom of God. *See*, Alan F. Johnson, *1 Corinthians, vol. 7, The IVP New Testament Commentary Series* (Westmont: IVP Academic, 2004), 98.
[197] Ibid., 747.
[198] Heb. 12:14 (NIV).

this life. Hebrews reminds us that *when* we come into the presence of God to worship, we come as the spirits of the righteous made perfect.[199] But this is also in anticipation that "nothing unclean shall enter into the presence of the heavenly city."[200] This demonstrates that our sinful thoughts and bodily practices cannot exist within the new Jerusalem.

The Apostle Paul also reveals, "At His coming, we will be made alive with a resurrection body and then we shall fully bear the image of the Man of Heaven."[201] In other words, we're getting to a place where we are Holy and blameless before the Lord, but we won't fully get there until we go to be with Him in heaven. Which is why Jesus had to be someone who knew no sin but became sin for us because we could not appear righteous before the Almighty by our own merits.

*God's Sovereignty Amidst Affliction*

I used to anguish over what God's will was for me. Should I stay at a church that I wasn't that happy with? Should I pursue a career outside of the church? Did I just spend seven years in Bible College and Seminary for nothing? Satan had placed all of these thoughts in my mind at one point or another over the past seven years, yet, I've discovered that every circumstance that God has put me in, *is* a part of His will because it either made me change direction in the course of my life, or it gave me the experience that I needed to open the next door that God had previously locked. Either way, God gets the glory for my achievements or setbacks, and in His glory, I have a human will that can choose to learn from it, reject it, embrace it, or change course because of it. The Bible says, "In their hearts, humans plan their course, but the LORD establishes their steps."[202] Simon Chan once wrote on this very subject:

First, a person who is really concerned about God's will is probably already in it. The willingness and desire after God *is* the will of God. Second, making a mistake in one choice does not mean forever missing out on God's perfect will...Third, the wrong choice may be the very means that God is using to bring the Christian to the place of contrition and humili-

[199] Heb. 12:23 (Emphasis mine).
[200] Rev. 21:27 (Emphasis mine).
[201] 1 Cor. 15:23-49 (Emphasis mine).
[202] Prov. 16:9 (NIV).

ty.[203]

Sometimes, when we think we're experiencing satanic affliction, God is using that experience to grow our faith and trust in Him. One of my theology professors used to say, "Don't think I'm a heretic, but I believe that God uses Satan as His bulldog." Maybe so, but certainly one could argue that the enemy has his own motivations for demonic affliction. Ignatius of Loyola once said, "Spiritual comfort comes from the Lord, while spiritual distress is from the evil spirit."[204] Therefore, discerning the spirits is of the utmost importance. How do we discern them? Look at the source.

The Old Testament Prophet, Jonah experienced a storm that was definitely sent by God. "Then the LORD sent a great wind on the sea, and such a violent storm arose that the ship threatened to break up."[205] God sent a violent storm because Jonah refused to sail to Nineveh and share God's message with the people who lived there.

Yet, in stark contrast, when the disciples were in the violent Sea of Galilee, Jesus rebuked the storm and questioned the disciples' faith.[206] Satan sent this storm to try and prevent Jesus from restoring a demon-possessed man, raising a girl from the dead, healing a sick woman, and allowing Him and His disciples to share the gospel message.[207] Jesus could not have rebuked Himself or the Father. So, we must remember that not all storms are sent by God; one storm was sent in response to man's disobedience, and one storm was sent in an attempt to prevent God's will. Yet, despite Satan's greatest efforts, God's will was still accomplished.

An example of where both God's will and our free will fuse together is in the book of Acts, chapter two:

> *Brothers, I may say to you with confidence about the patriarch David that he both died and was buried, and his tomb is with us to this day...God had sworn with an oath to him that he would set one of his descendants on his throne, he foresaw and spoke about the resurrection of the Christ...This Jesus God raised up, and of that we are all witnesses...This Jesus whom YOU cru-*

---

[203] Chan, *Spiritual Theology*, 201.
[204] Ignatius, quoted in Chan, *Spiritual Theology*, 204.
[205] Jonah 1:4 (NIV).
[206] See Mark 4:35-41.
[207] See Mark Chapter Five.

*cified!* [208]

Did you catch it? Here, Peter has just explained how Jesus links to King David by God's sovereign foreknowledge and will, and in the same breath, tells them they crucified Him! Meaning, that they *chose* to crucify the Christ who was already in God's plan to die for our sins. Isn't that amazing? Again, despite Satan's efforts, God's will has still prevailed. Had they not crucified Christ; we would not be able to enjoy eternity with the Father. And, that is what we need to always remember. There is a constant juxtaposition in the spiritual realm between God's sovereignty and our free will, yet both advance God's good purposes. Some theologians define this as, "God's hidden will."

Recently, I've been thinking about the COVID-19 pandemic in light of free will. Each of us has a responsibility to be obedient to the Father, but my lack of obedience might affect others' quest in their obedience to God. So, let's say, hypothetically, I choose to disobey the warnings against public gatherings, and gather anyways. Yet, God has clearly put it upon my heart not to disobey this order. This may indeed result in someone catching the virus from me, (perhaps I'm an unknown carrier) when I might have prevented infecting someone else by simply listening to the Holy Spirit. Of course, the other side of the coin is that God would allow Satan to encourage me to ignore the Holy Spirit to advance His greater purpose of somebody catching the virus from me, according to God's hidden will. Now you might realize, by reading this simplistic example, why this paradox has never been fully resolved.

*Conclusion*

Fundamentally, we must realize that we are in a constant battle with the enemy. These are demonic forces unseen. Not only should we be ready for the psychological battles, but also, we need to be proactive in our process of growth in Christ. Sanctification is truly a life-long process. Stand firm in God's armor and use the Sword of the Spirit to go on the offensive, prior to any spiritual battle. God's Word will cut deep into the enemy's foothold, for Satan must yield to the name above all names; the name of Jesus Christ.

---

[208] Acts 2:29-36 (Emphasis mine).

# CHAPTER 5

## The Power of Prayer

No spiritual formation book would be complete without a section on prayer. Prayer holds so much power, if we only realized it. Jesus prayed all night before choosing His disciples (see Luke 6:12). Jesus also prayed in anguish right before His betrayal (see Matthew 26:36-56). Matthew chapter six contains the prayer that Jesus modeled to His disciples, and prayer that extends to us, which is commonly known as, *The Lord's Prayer* (see Matt. 6:9-13).

One of the best books that I've read on the Lord's prayer is, *Fifty-Seven Words that Change the World* by Darrell W. Johnson. There are so many great insights in that book that it's hard to list them all, but I think the revelation that struck me most was when Johnson noted that the Lord's Prayer encompasses all of time.[209] This realization hadn't occurred to me before while reading or reciting the Lord's prayer. Looking at the past, we often seek forgiveness; looking at the present, we all need sustenance, and finally, looking towards the future, we seek protection from all that may harm or tempt us.[210] The Lord's Prayer is fully comprehensive and inclusive; nothing is left out.

*Our Father Who Art in Heaven*

---

[209] Johnson, *Fifty-Seven Words That Change the World*, 16.
[210] Ibid.

The opening to the Lord's Prayer reminds us that our Father is in Heaven at all times, yet He is also around us at all times, intimately involved in our life because God is very relational. The Word still dwells among us and is very loving towards us, like a Father should be to His children.

The phrase, "Our Father in heaven," which is not bound by space and time, accounts for the immediate heavens as well as distant heavens. Genesis 1:1 records the word "heaven" in the plural (heavens), not the singular. Jesus says, "I am the Alpha and the Omega, the First and the Last, the Beginning and the End."[211] Therefore, He exists everywhere and at all times. This is extremely comforting because unlike us, who are bound by space and time, God is omnipresent and can be all places at all times. This means He is listening to you and me right this very moment. What are you going to say to Him?

*Hallowed be Thy Name*

God ought to be exalted and lifted up at all times in faithful worship. I spend many hours a day thinking about how magnificent the Father is and how many great things He's created all around me. When I drive into the mountains of Lake Tahoe, I worship Him by speaking my adoration of the beauty that surrounds me. Why should I exalt Him? Because He is the creator of all of heaven and earth; the universe and everything in it. The Father permits me to wake up every morning, and for that, I am forever grateful.

God's name was first revealed through the burning bush to Moses. Yet, "I Am" can also be interpreted relationally.[212] I have always preached that "I Am" transcends time by being a verb in the present tense; however, God's name may better be interpreted as, *I am there with you*, or, *I am there for you*.

---

[211] Rev. 22:13 (NIV).
[212] Johnson, *Fifty-Seven Words That Change the World*, 35.

*Thy Kingdom Come, Thy Will be Done*

We must consider that the Lord is the King and we are His subjects. We should be willing to recognize that it's important to always place reverence upon God at all times because if we do not, then we lower Him to our human standards instead of trying to elevate ourselves to His.

The term "Kingdom of God" does not reflect a specific location, but rather that God is acting as king.[213] As mentioned earlier, God is not limited to space and time; therefore, the kingdom cannot be limited to those boundaries either. The concept of realized eschatology/preterist doctrine demonstrates how Jesus ushered in the kingdom (see Luke 17:20-21), yet we know that the future kingdom has yet to take place (see Luke 19:11-12) so, the kingdom of heaven itself is not somewhere we travel to, but rather something that we embrace inside of us once we accept Jesus Christ into our hearts.

Some may wish that God's will wasn't so, or that we must participate in His will, only begrudgingly. Yet, God is sovereign, and His will is manifested as such. "Your will be done," means your purpose and pleasure be done; your design and delight be done."[214] This is why it is important to pray with thanksgiving and praise (Psalm 100:4, emphasis mine) because, in actuality, we are humbly thanking God for what He has already decided upon.

*On Earth, as It Is in Heaven*

We need to consider that what is already being done in Heaven should be mirrored here on earth. God has everything in order and without sin in the heavenly realm so we must work on being more Christ-like in our efforts to honor the Holy One because if we do not separate ourselves from the world, then we are no different than anyone else who proclaims to be a "good person," yet fails to demonstrate goodness in their hearts.

---

[213] Ibid., 43.
[214] Ibid., 56.

*Give Us This Day our Daily Bread*

This petition should remind us that God sustains our physical life as well as our spiritual one. We must remember that the Father is constantly providing for us in one way or another; without the Father sustaining us, we would be given over to the hands of the enemy, both physically and spiritually, so we must integrate thanksgiving for His provisions regularly.

I concur with Martin Luther and his interpretation of the fourth petition of praying for daily bread. "The bread" goes beyond physical nourishment; it includes all of life's provisions. This makes sense because when we pray for it, we are not limiting the prayer to only ourselves. The 1st person plural pronouns "us" and "our" indicate that all children of God need these heavenly provisions to survive.

*Forgive Us Our Debts as We Have also Forgiven our Debtors*

This petition is a great reminder that forgiveness is very important to God. We are debt-free thanks to Jesus Christ who paid our debts for us on the cross. Jesus forgave us, so we must also forgive others because if we lack forgiveness, then we let bitterness and anger eat away at us which impacts our relationship with God, and our relationship with others. We have an obligation to first ask forgiveness from our Father, then ask forgiveness from the image-bearers that we have sinned against.

There is a powerful correlation between Jesus' response to Peter about the number of times we should forgive someone (seventy-seven times), and Lamech's song that ends, "If Cain is avenged seven times, then Lamech seventy-seven times" (*Gen. 4:24*). I have read the Pentateuch hundreds of times and totally missed this connection. The "seven" and "seventy-seven" numbers speak of the reversal of the natural human tendency towards resentment and revenge.[215] So, no longer is the forgiveness limitation set at 490 times per occurrence, but rather, we should forgive others in an unlimited fashion, and at all times because if we don't, we will only harbor resentment and bitterness inside of us.

---

[215] Ibid., 81.

# The Power of Prayer

*Lead Us Not into Temptation, but Deliver Us From (the) Evil (one)*

When we pray, "Lead us not into temptation, but deliver us from evil," we are actually asking, "let not God's trials become Satan's temptations." This is because the Greek word for trial and temptation is the same (πειρασμός) and the Greek adjective "evil" is functioning as a substantial adjective meaning that it should translate as evil one.[216] We know that God puts us through trials and tribulations, but the question is, do we allow Satan to turn God's trials into Satan's temptations that separate us from God, or do we get closer to God by trusting in Him after we persevere through the trial? The choice is always ours.

The two clauses of the sixth petition of the Lord's Prayer are tied together by using the conjunction, "but." Again, the idea is that what we are asking is not that the Father prevents us from Satan's temptation, but that He prevents the test from becoming a temptation of Satan.[217] God tests us to increase our faith. One might argue that life itself is one big test. Will we pass, or will we fail? Sadly, many will fail, but I find that the tests that God has put me through have always improved my relationship with Him. Sometimes, I have to look back on my life to appreciate it.

When reciting the Lord's Prayer, it is important to remember that God is a loving Father who only wants the best for us. Unlike some earthly fathers, our heavenly Father has no flaws, abusive tendencies, anger issues, or substance abuse problems. He is what we as earthly fathers should strive to imitate. Like our earthly fathers, God may get upset when we go against His commands for us. He may get heated when we worship other gods, He may destroy the idols we worship, but that's because He loves us and wants what is best for us. Humans run into trouble when we go against God's design. Fortunately, He loved us enough to reconcile us back to Himself through His son, Jesus Christ.

---

[216] Ibid., 92.
[217] Ibid., 93.

*For Thine is the Kingdom, and the Power, and the Glory, Forever and Ever, Amen*

This doxology demonstrates that God controls and dwells in His Kingdom, He has all power and glory, and that He deserves full reverence and respect. These truths should be encouraging because this is a proclamation of God's greatness which reminds us to always revere and honor Him.

*The High Priestly Prayer*

Perhaps, the most powerful prayer is delivered by Jesus, Himself in John chapter seventeen:

*Jesus Prays to Be Glorified*

After Jesus said this, he looked toward heaven and prayed:

> Father, the hour has come. Glorify your Son, that your Son may glorify you. For you granted him authority over all people that he might give eternal life to all those you have given him. Now, this is eternal life: that they know you, the only true God, and Jesus Christ, whom you have sent. I have brought you glory on earth by finishing the work you gave me to do. And now, Father, glorify me in your presence with the glory I had with you before the world began.

*Jesus Prays for His Disciples*

> 'I have revealed you to those whom you gave me out of the world. They were yours; you gave them to me, and they have obeyed your word. Now they know that everything you have given me comes from you. For I gave them the words you gave me, and they accepted them. They knew with certainty that I came from you, and they believed that you sent me. I pray for them. I am not praying for the world, but for those you have given me, for they are yours. All I have is yours, and all you have is mine. And glory has come to me through them. I will remain in the world no longer, but they are still in the world, and I am coming to you. Holy Father protect them by the power of your name, the name you gave me, so that they may be one as we are one. While I was with them, I protected them and kept them safe by that name you gave me. None has been lost except the one doomed to destruction so that Scripture would be fulfilled.'

> 'I am coming to you now, but I say these things while I am still in the world, so that they may have the full measure of my joy within them. I have given them

*your word and the world has hated them, for they are not of the world any more than I am of the world. My prayer is not that you take them out of the world but that you protect them from the evil one. They are not of the world, even as I am not of it. Sanctify them by the truth; your word is truth. As you sent me into the world, I have sent them into the world. For them, I sanctify myself, that they too may be truly sanctified.'*

*Jesus Prays for All Believers*

*'My prayer is not for them alone. I pray also for those who will believe in me through their message, that all of them may be one, Father, just as you are in me and I am in you. May they also be in us so that the world may believe that you have sent me. I have given them the glory that you gave me, that they may be one as we are one—I in them and you in me—so that they may be brought to complete unity. Then the world will know that you sent me and have loved them even as you have loved me. Father, I want those you have given me to be with me where I am, and to see my glory, the glory you have given me because you loved me before the creation of the world. Righteous Father, though the world does not know you, I know you, and they know that you have sent me. I have made you known to them and will continue to make you known in order that the love you have for me may be in them and that I myself may be in them.*[218]

Jesus' prayer in John chapter seventeen is very powerful because it demonstrates the longing for unity that Jesus has for us, as He, Himself is unified with the Father. Upon initial observation of verses one through five, it seems apparent that Jesus and the Father are glorified together by Jesus' selfless act on the cross. Additionally, did you notice that Jesus proclaims the glory He had with the Father before the world began? I believe that this relates to Proverbs chapter eight, in which Jesus is personified as, "The wisdom of God."[219]

---

[218] John 17:1-26 (NIV).

[219] See Prov. 8:22-36. Contrasted with sensual allurements are the advantages of divine wisdom, which publicly invites men, offers the best principles of life, and the most valuable benefits resulting from receiving her counsels. Her relation to the divine plans and acts is introduced, as in Prov. 3:19, 20, though more fully, to commend her desirableness for men, and the whole is closed by an assurance that those finding her find God's favor, and those neglecting ruin themselves. *Many regards the passage as a description of the Son of God by the title, Wisdom, which the older Jews used (and by which He is called in Lu 11:49), as Jn 1:1, &c., describes Him*

In verses six through nineteen, Jesus prays for His disciples. It's beautiful to read that Jesus prayed for protection from the Evil One, and for those who remained faithful to Him and were still in the world. They were indeed, the first to follow as well as the first to give their lives in the name of Jesus Christ.

Lastly, Jesus prays for all believers, including us, that we may be unified with the Father and the Son, and through the power of the Holy Spirit, that we can still be with Jesus where He is. The love that is in the Father and Son is also in us.

*Prayer Contemplations*

I had the honor of taking a prayer course by Dr. Calvin Blom in Seminary a year ago. It really transformed my life because it unlocked some of the messages that the Holy Spirit was trying to tell me but couldn't fully hear. After all, I never took the additional time needed to listen to Him. I've included one of my directed prayer contemplations below:

*September 16th, 2019*

The first thing that I do, even before my Scripture meditation, is to "set the stage." I often do this because it helps me to invite God's presence into a welcoming environment. For me, setting the stage represents the aesthetic components of the prayer experience. I chose to set the stage by communing with the Father in His beautiful creation. I drove to a nearby

---

*by that of Logos, the Word.* But the passage may be taken as a personification of wisdom: for, (1) Though described as with God, wisdom is not asserted to be God. (2) The use of personal attributes is equally consistent with a *personification,* as with the description of a real person. (3) The personal pronouns used accord with the gender (feminine) of wisdom constantly, and are never changed to that of the person meant, as sometimes occurs in a corresponding use of *spirit,* which is neuter in *Greek,* but to which masculine pronouns are often applied (Jn 16:14), when the acts of the Holy Spirit are described. (4) Such a personification is agreeable to the style of this book (compare Pr 1:20; 4:8; 6:20–22; 9:1–4), whereas no prophetical or other allusions to the Savior or the new dispensation are found among the quotations of this book in the New Testament, and unless this be such, none exist. (5) Nothing is lost as to the importance of this passage, which still remains a most ornate and also solemn and impressive teaching of inspiration on the value of wisdom. *See,* Robert Jamieson, A. R. Fausset, and David Brown, *Commentary Critical and Explanatory on the Whole Bible,* vol. 1 (Oak Harbor, WA: Logos Research Systems, Inc., 1997), 393.

walking trail along the Truckee River and sat on a bench there just watching the water for two hours.

I spent twenty minutes meditating over each of the six passages in Mark, as suggested by the exercise. As usual, Satan was not patient in trying to distract me, so I simply rebuked him and commanded him to get behind me. It's amazing what the Lord will reveal to you if you simply direct your thoughts and prayers into specific passages of Scripture.

In reading Mark 7:5-13, The Lord spoke to my heart and mentioned that we often use excuses for where our money is prioritized. In other words, I might say I'm honoring my mother and father by spending money on them while they are healthy, yet in their time of need, I might choose to place them in a retirement home because it's much more convenient for me. This very situation happened with my grandmother when she went into hospice. My family would have rather paid for hospice to care for her in her final days than sacrifice the time and money to care for her themselves.

Quoting from Isaiah, καρδία (heart) is used in the Greek to describe the distance between honoring God with the lips and honoring God with the heart. καρδία is where we get the word cardiology from, yet the Greeks often used it to mean, "inner self." Indeed, where your treasure is, there your heart will be also (see Matt. 6:21).

Mark 7:14-21 also deals with the heart. I'm pleasantly reminded that I can be around defilement and not let it consume me. I once listened to an illustration by a young pastor in Chicago who said that when he goes to eat sushi, the fish does not taste overly salty, even though the fish lives in the ocean its entire life, is covered in salt, and even breathes salt in and out of its gills constantly. That's because the fish is not consumed by its environment. The same can be applied to us regarding sin. We are surrounded by sin at all times, but we do not have to let our environments consume us.

Mark 10:17-23 really spoke to me. How many times have I read this passage? Hundreds, thousands? Suddenly, I received a revelation, and perhaps some support for my thoughts on free will. You see, the rich man had a choice to sell all of his possessions; his earthly "gods," and enjoy eternity with the everlasting one, Jesus Christ. Much like Adam, the rich man rejected God's offer and chose dependence upon something else. And, so it is with our salvation, God will often initiate our relationship with Him, yet we still have a choice to accept the invitation or choose to worship something else, sadly many choose the latter. I thank God that He chose me, and I accepted Him in return.

For me, this passage isn't so much about the rich man's possessions and having a hard time parting with them, it's about rejecting God's offer of salvation. Notice the rich man's question, *what must I do to inherit eternal life?* [220] This is the same as asking, *how do I get salvation?* Jesus wasn't saying if you sell everything you will "earn" your way into heaven; Jesus was saying that if you cannot part ways with your idols, i.e. money, then you cannot glorify God and trust in His Son for eternal life. So, like Adam in the Garden, the rich man rejected God's (Jesus') offer of salvation (eternal life) by rejecting the covenant that He was trying to make with him. And, indeed, Adam began to die, both physically, and spiritually.

Now, I'm not inferring that Adam isn't currently in heaven, but in that particular moment, just like in that particular moment of the rich man's life, he was literally rejecting what God was offering to him. It's quite possible, that later in his life, the rich man realized that money was not a god to be worshiped and perhaps turned to Jesus and accepted Him into his heart before the rich man died. The Scripture doesn't give us the end of the story. But the Bible does tell us what we must do to be saved: *If you declare with your mouth, 'Jesus is Lord,' and believe in your heart that God raised him from the dead, you will be saved.* [221]

In summary, this was a beautiful experience for me overall. I tend to be an emotional person and so I found myself tearing up quite a bit. I learned that one of the main challenges I have is not to allow what I've learned in my seven and a half years of formal theological education to influence my meditation in a particular moment with God. In turn, I learned that God will speak if we take the time to listen to Him. In the process of communing with God, I realized that His grace is sufficient for my needs; I simply have to ask that He reveal that to me. God spoke to me in several ways during this prayer time. His words are always valuable, and I look forward to the next time we speak with each other.

---

[220] Mark 10:17 (NIV).
[221] Rom. 10:9 (NIV).

Richard Foster highlights adoration prayer in his book, simply titled, *Prayer.* According to Foster, "When our reply to God is most direct of all, it is called *adoration.* Adoration is the spontaneous yearning of the heart to worship, honor, magnify, and bless God."[222] I think that adoration is the highest form of prayer, and one in which I've experienced some amazing revelation. Once, I was exalting God and praying about the Holy Sprit's role in our advocacy to the Father. This is what I recorded in my communication with God journal:

> *I awoke at 4 am this morning and was in prayer half asleep about what is the role of the Holy Spirit if Jesus intercedes for us? I know He is our "helper/teacher" or paraclete, but does He do more than that? The Lord told me, "You better write this down or Satan will make you forget it." The following is dictated from what The Lord told me in my mind to write down. "Jesus intercedes for us for our salvation, but the Holy Spirit intercedes for us against our flesh. For if The Spirit isn't in constant intercession, the flesh would tear us away from The Holy One"*
> ~The Lord (4:30 am 3/15/2014)

Lastly, it's important to write out a prayer to the Lord and recite it regularly for an extended duration. Watch how God will answer your prayer every single day. He certainly did for me when I recited these two prayers each day, morning, and evening for a one-month period:

*Personal Morning and Evening Prayer*

*Morning Prayer:*

Thank you for another beautiful morning today, LORD. You are magnificent in all ways. My heart desires that I get to know you more as this day progresses. Please shield my heart from the temptations of today and help me to help someone else who needs to hear from you. In Jesus' Holy name,
Amen.

---

[222] Foster, *Prayer,* 81.

*Evening Prayer:*

Dear LORD, I ask your forgiveness for my disobedience towards you, and I thank you for another opportunity to glorify you tomorrow. Please allow your peace to pour over me as I sleep and please protect my family and friends from the arrows of the enemy. Thank you for having mercy on me and thank you for loving me unconditionally. In Jesus' Holy name, Amen.

*Meditation and Reflection*

Part of my graduate studies in Spiritual Formation at Multnomah University involved spending alone time with God on four separate occasions and reflecting on those experiences. I had the honor of immersing myself in God's glowing presence during those reflections a few years ago. Sometimes, all we need to do is sit in silence and wait for God to speak to us. He may not speak audibly, but He will surely speak into our thoughts and into our hearts. Be careful though, for Satan will try and take that precious time away from you with his own influences. The following are my personal reflections after spending four hours with the Father in silence:

*Reflection One*

Dark clouds and choppy waters inhabit the atmosphere as soft raindrops fall on the cold cement ground at the marina in Sparks, Nevada. I cannot help but think of my savior and the many storms that He conquered for us as I peer out into the openness of His mighty creation. He tells me to remain steadfast and to stay with the plan that has been provided for me since the foundation of the world. There were many times when I felt I couldn't persevere; that a life of serving Him was too hard. "Keep the faith, my child, He says, for I have great plans to prosper you. Many before you and many after you will have given up on my plan. It is vital that you persevere," says the Lord Almighty. The Lord was there with me in the past, and He dwells with me now. There is no escaping the Lord's presence; there is no hiding from His almighty power.

One thing that I learned about myself during this time is that I feel the most connected to God when I take time out to let Him speak to me. He's always there to listen and always there to advise. I tend to overanalyze experiences or daily events in my life. When I look out at God's creation, I'm overwhelmed by the fact that His omniscience is ever increasing. At times, I can be too confident; too prideful. His omnipotence causes me to cast the glory upon Him instead of myself.

I realized that I don't have all the answers to life's questions. I need to depend more upon God to direct my steps. Sometimes, I try and conquer my demons alone. Only through His strength can they be truly defeated. The Apostle Peter began to sink when he took his eyes off of Jesus Christ. I too can fall into deep despair when I lose focus on who matters most.

I discovered that God is very loving, kind, compassionate, and encouraging. I experienced tremendous encouragement as doubts by the enemy began to set in. God is wonderful. He reminded me of the various times in which He rescued me from certain dangers. He created flashbacks in my memory to times of sorrow and despair in which His light remained shining upon me through the power of the Holy Spirit. He reassured me that He still tabernacles within me and that I need to remain on guard, bearing my Spiritual armor, for Satan is constantly trying to separate me from the Holy One.

*Reflection Two*

God has never forsaken me. He loves me just as much when I fall back as when I step forward in faith. He is not impressed with my earthly accomplishments, but rather, what moves Him is the love that I have for one another. By shining His light into this dark world, I create unity between us. This is what I live for; this is what I will die for. God's love for me is beyond measure. When I doubt how much He loves me, I merely need to look up at the cross.

I learned that the process of working through these four hours was not so much about what I need, but rather, what God desires from me. God has blessed me so much in this life, the least I can do is honor and glorify Him throughout my journey. God is always ready to listen, but I must also allow Him to speak.

I struggled in letting my past sins and defeat reemerge to convince me that I cannot persevere. I had moments of doubt, lack of faith, and questions as to my purpose in this life. Yet, through God's love and mercy, He reminded me that my sins have been forgiven; that I live in a broken world in which He has already put a plan in motion to restore. He encouraged me that I must live as a saint who sins, not as a sinner trying to become a saint.

Through faith in Him, I will always emerge victoriously.

I discovered that by having a new identity in Jesus Christ, I have already defeated Satan; now I must live like it. These four hours were very powerful. God has truly spoken to my heart through this experience. I plan on spending alone time with God more often throughout my life. If I can be still and listen to His voice, I can accomplish all things with He who dwells in me.

*Reflection Three*

In the silent lucidity of my home in North West Reno, I contemplate a much simpler time in which my faith was unchallenged; even unquestioned. Peering out of my windows, I can see God move through His tapestry in the clouds. God's canvas of sunrises, sunsets, rain, and snow provides for the perfect backdrop to the glorious lake and mountains that surround Sierra Nevada.

The Father is using this time to address my issues of pride and needing acceptance from an unforgiving world. "Remain humble," I can hear Him say. "For in humility, my Son died for you." Indeed, He did. Jesus Christ remained obedient and humble His entire life up to and including His death on a cross.

I need you, oh Lord, how I need you. Your love never fails, never gives up, and never gives out on me. Time marches forward, yet you remain there, deep within me, and several steps ahead of me. You are the great I AM. Once again, I've discovered your compassion, your quickness to forgive, and your support through this journey towards Christlikeness.

I can feel your presence in the form of the Holy Spirit as I say a blessing for each room of my home. In the stillness of the night, I awake to discover a tugging on my heart to pray against the powers and principalities of the Evil One; to dispel the darkness that inhabits this place of light. My God is mighty to save; He provides my every need. From the time I wake up in the morning, throughout my day, and lastly, when I go to bed at night, the Lord is sustaining the very life; the very breath that I take. Life itself cannot exist apart from Him. I need to continue to work on building a lasting relationship with the Father through prayer, fellowship, meditation, reading His Word, and solitude.

Focusing on Him and His plan for me will give my life meaning and purpose. Too often, I try and set my own destiny but fail to realize that God is more than willing to guide me in the right direction. I have yet to face a hardship that God has not helped me get through. It's during the trials and tribulations of my life, that God strengthens me for the next challenge. My wife and beautiful children are all gifts from Him. I pray that He will continue to care for and protect my children long after I've left this world. Like the mind of a child, we must be willing to put full faith and trust in the Father. By infusing God's values and worldview into my children, they too will develop a loving relationship with the Holy One. Feeling the conviction of the Spirit to focus more on my wife and children, God has spoken to me once again during this quiet time with Him. My children are only little for a little while, I must share more about my faith and principles with them before the enemy can enter their minds bringing fear, divisiveness, and separation. I must continue to pray diligently for their spiritual wellbeing as well as my own.

*Reflection Four*

As the rain begins to fall and absorb into the earth, the Holy Spirit speaks into my heart inviting me to allow God to transform me into the image of His Son. Christ Jesus is the one who was, who is, and who is to come. No longer am I judged by the world's standards, but rather, by God's standards which He holds so high that earthly beings cannot attain them. Only through my faith and trust in Jesus Christ, can the Father see me as the finished product. Like the incense that once burned in the Holy of Holies to block God's view of the sin within the person dwelling there, I am now seen through the lens of Christ, and not of the world.

Spirit lead me to walk in the light and shield me from the darkness. Christ has paid the price for sin once and for all, so I am no longer bound by it; I am no longer held prisoner by it. Thank you, God, for your patience with me. Thank you for forgiving me when I fall back. Thank you for your Son for dying for me. Thank you for your Spirit for dwelling within me. I love you with all of my heart, mind, soul, and strength.

*Conclusion*

Prayer is tremendously important in our walk with Christ. Paul tells us to, "Pray in the Spirit at all times."[223] This means we must rely and depend upon Him for how we pray. I pray every single night before I go to sleep; thanking God for what He's done in my life and in the lives of my family and friends. I thank Him for allowing me to live another day to worship and glorify Him. I ask for His protection against the enemy, against the powers and principalities that are unseen, and against the impure thoughts that often enter into my mind. Then I fall asleep; soundly, knowing that God's Spirit is alive and well, igniting the fire inside of me once again.

---

[223] Eph. 6:18 (Emphasis mine).

# CHAPTER 6

## Growing into Christ's Likeness

When I was very young, I did household chores like most kids my age. I remember that often, I would have to do the same chore more than once. This was because my stepfather was very meticulous and perhaps, somewhat of a perfectionist, when it came to doing tasks. I always detested doing something twice and eventually learned to do it right the first time. As I grew older, I found myself expecting the same from my children; maybe with a little less intensity though. You could say, I grew into my stepfather's likeness, at least as it pertained to accuracy and efficiency. Jesus adds to this sentiment as well by stating, "The student is not above the teacher, but everyone who is fully trained will be like their teacher."[224]

Regarding my own growth in spiritual formation, I work very hard at maintaining a strong and healthy relationship with the Lord. I attempt to make a consorted effort to pray fervently and with focus every single day. Harmonizing soul care with spiritual direction enables me to overcome fleshly temptations that detach me from the Father. By meditating on God's Word day and night, I am inviting the Holy Spirit to strengthen my bond with Him. I continue to nurture my relationship with Jesus Christ by living the Spirit-led life that He modeled so well when He once walked among us.

---

[224] Luke 6:40 (NIV).

By seeking first, the kingdom of God, we allow the Holy Spirit to guide our choices. If we better recognize our mental triggers, we can resist the devil at the onset of his temptations. We must continue to guard the light inside of us that shines so bright in this dark world, and by utilizing the Holy Spirit, we can bolster our hearts against many earthly temptations.

It's important to have a strong love for mankind. It is essential to guard this strength because God loves His creation even more than we do. When we feel hurt or betrayed by others, we should remember how Jesus reacted to those who tried to harm Him; not in vengeance, but love. In the event that we forget ourselves and our purpose in this life, we must look toward the cross and remember the love that God had for us on it.

Being in God's presence is imperative. The ability for us to allow His words to speak into our hearts must be fortified at all times. We must make a better effort in escaping the pandemonium of everyday life and allow the Holy Spirit to speak to us. Be quick to listen and slow to speak, for in the stillness of the night, God's voice echoes within our souls.

An essential aspect of growing into Christlikeness is to practice self-control. Paul lists self-control as one of the fruits of the Spirit (see Gal. 5:22-23) that we should all possess as believers. Self-control is one of the most challenging disciplines when dealing with the temptations of the flesh, but it can be done if we rely upon the power of the Holy Spirit to guide us in resisting temptation.

When I struggled with promiscuity in my early to mid twenties, I felt pungently condemned for not being able to control my obsessions. I suffered a strong sense of shame brought on by the enemy and begged the Lord for His forgiveness. As the Holy Spirit empowered me to achieve better self-control in this area of my life, the Lord no longer let Satan condemn me when I fell back; instead, the Lord lovingly told me, "Let's get this under control before you end up really hurting someone." It didn't take me long to realize that, that someone… was me.

In addition to self-control, we also need to take better care of our bodies. Our bodies are temples of God; we have a duty to work on cleansing them. Physically, we should exercise more frequently and eat healthier foods. Spiritually, we must continue to wear God's armor. The sword of the Spirit is our best form of offense in combatting the evil around us.

We can always be better at bearing one another's burdens. In my haste, I tend to overlook some of the struggles of my brothers and sisters in the faith. Lovingly, take the time to pray, comfort, and offer support and guidance to those that are suffering around us. By offering my support to others in need, I can show the love of Christ, not only through my words but also through my actions.

One way in which I work on my spiritual transformation is to study those who have transformed before me. Many theologians who were alive during the Classical Antiquity period of the Greco-Roman world, have preserved their writings and prayer journals for us to enjoy and to learn from. In my readings, I have discovered that the early Patristic Father, Irenaeus, had actually been discipled by Polycarp. In the line of apostolic succession, Polycarp comes second under the Apostle John. Polycarp was so solid in his faith that he dared to scold the Roman proconsul for not accepting Jesus Christ as Lord, even while being burned at the stake!

Irenaeus was one of the first spiritual sailors (besides the Apostle John) to associate the term λόγος (logos) with Jesus Christ. Jesus, having been God incarnate, is in fact the divine logos, or *reasoning* in which early Christians could identify Christ with.[225] This philosophy ties in nicely with the wisdom personification in Proverbs chapter eight verses twelve through thirty-six.

As mentioned in chapter two, another early church Father who was very influential was Origen. In my opinion, Origen gets somewhat of a bad rap for his spiritual philosophy. Certainly, associating every single Scripture with some type of allegory or deeper message is hermeneutically irresponsible; however, there are obvious allegorical passages in the Bible, namely, Jesus' parables, which often compare one thing to another, use a rhetorical device, clever metaphor, or agricultural allegory to point toward a larger message.

Many biblical scholars view the Book of Jonah as an allegory or Old Testament parable. So, there is some merit to Origen's claims. The danger occurs when Scripture is not used to interpret Scripture. The very definition

---

[225] Schmidt, *God Seekers*, 5.

of an allegory is *the expression by means of symbolic figures and actions of truths or generalizations about human existence; a symbolic representation.*[226]

A good example of an allegory in which Scripture does interpret Scripture is the story of Moses striking the Rock in the Book of Exodus. Many would claim that the Rock represents Christ who provides life-giving water, and many would be correct. The symbolism for Christ as the Rock of Horeb is a justified allegory because the Apostle Paul interprets it for us in 1 Corinthians: "They all ate the same spiritual food and drank the same spiritual drink; for they drank from the spiritual rock that accompanied them, and that rock was Christ."[227]

I've always been intrigued by the early monastics. Possibly one of the first monks in the history of Christianity was none other than Antony, who was known as "The Father of Christian Monasticism."[228] Antony spent many years in the solitude of the desert in prayer, fasting, and meditation. One of the benefits of living in solitude is that there are no distractions that may hinder one's connection with Christ and the Holy Spirit; however, excessive time in solitude can often lead the devil to attack the weaknesses of those closest to Christ. A balance of the two proficiencies is the best option for those working on spiritual formation/care.

Not long after Christianity was legalized by the Edict of Milan, the Church began structuring itself as more of a formal entity within Cappadocia. Religion and politics began making their collaborative debut as titles were given to the Cappadocian elite upper class of "Bishop and Archbishop." Ironically, two of the Cappadocian fathers wanted little to do with running the church of the East.[229] Sadly, Gregory of Nyssa was a universalist, much like Origen, yet God used the Cappadocian Fathers to help draft the Nicene Creed, in which the divinity of Christ was firmly established.[230] Gregory of Nyssa emphasized that God is relationship. Indeed, God is not only in relationship with His creation, but He is also in relationship within Himself in the form of the Holy Trinity.

---

[226] Merriam-Webster, s.v. "Allegory," accessed May 18, 2020, https://www.merriam-webster.com/dictionary/allegory.

[227] 1 Cor. 10:3-4 (NIV).

[228] Schmidt, *God Seekers*, 24.

[229] Ibid., 36.

[230] Ibid., 39.

All of these early church Fathers had genuine experiences with Jesus Christ, whether that be in a monastery, in the desert, or burning at the stake. Some held to orthodox theological positions, and some were more liberal in their theology. Unfortunately for them, unorthodox positions often led to death. However, my Patristics professor once said, "We mustn't be too hard on these patristic Fathers for their beliefs, because they might not be the ones who were wrong, we might be."[231]

By detaching ourselves from the world, we can better align ourselves with Christ. It is significant that we stay focused on *God's* approval and not *earthly* recognition of our achievements. Our satisfaction should be, not that we've approved of our deeds, but rather, that we've intimately sought-after Jesus Christ and cherished others to the best of our ability. By allowing for time in solitude with the Spirit, we can sharpen our inner-most thoughts and experience revelation like never before. Soaking in the beauty of God's creation in nature allows us to ponder some of life's bigger questions. Make the time to listen for the answers in that soft still voice that only the Spirit can yield.

By permitting ourselves to forgive others who have wronged us, we can experience God's forgiveness at the same time. By loving God with all of our heart, soul, strength, and mind, we can, in turn, love both our neighbor, and our self. In the end, what matters to me most in this life is that I was able to love, and to be loved.

*The Fully Mature Christian*

> *And I, brethren, could not speak to you as to spiritual men, but as to men of flesh, as to infants in Christ. I gave you milk to drink, not solid food; for you were not yet able to receive it. Indeed, even now you are not yet able, for you are still fleshly. For since there is jealousy and strife among you, are you not fleshly, and are you not walking like mere men? For when one says, "I am of Paul," and another, "I am of Apollos," are you not mere men? What then is Apollos? And what is Paul? Servants through whom you believed, even as the Lord gave opportunity to each one. I planted, Apollos watered, but God was causing the growth. So then neither the one who plants nor the one who waters is anything, but God who causes the growth. Now he who plants and he who waters*

---

[231] Professor Slavin, Patristics & Medieval Theology lecture, Sept. 2018.

*are one; but each will receive his own reward according to his own labor. For we are God's fellow workers; you are God's field, God's building.*[232]

Answering the call of every Christian implicates planting seeds. Some seeds fall on good soil, and some on rocky ground. We may indeed water the seeds, but God causes them to grow. Sometimes the harvest comes late. Sometimes you sow seeds of hope without really knowing it. And, still, sometimes the fruit of your labor comes in a way and time that you would never expect.

My daughter, Michelle, had accepted God's gift of salvation at a young age. But she never saw herself as some exceptional Christian who could change lives. She was just an eleven-year-old girl trying to cope with adolescence, school, and living under our roof and rules while balancing friendships—just a kid trying to live as God would want her to.

Yet, Michelle is also a very talented artist with a heart for God and other people. She gladly sits with me every Sunday morning as I conduct church services and is always eager to learn about God. She's happy to share the gospel message with anyone who will listen. Just living her life is a testimony of the great faith she has in Jesus Christ. I take no credit for Michelle's growth; God is causing her to grow, I'm just privileged to be the instrument that He's using to help accomplish that purpose.

All of us are writing a story with our lives—one that affects others now and in the future. Are we living to please God? Or are we living to please ourselves? At the time of this writing, Americans are currently quarantined in our homes due to COVID-19 (the Corona Virus of 2019). Though we cannot *physically* interact with each other as much as we'd like to, we can still *spiritually* interact with both God and with each other simultaneously.

We are witnessing God's golden fields of wheat begin to mature. His choice fruits begin to ripen; therefore, we should live every day with an eye on His harvest. The closer we get to Jesus Christ, the more fruit we bear. And, the more fruit we bear, the more we shine Christ's light into this dark world.

---

[232] 1 Cor. 3:1-9 (NASB).

In context, verses one through three of 1 Corinthians chapter three, talks about spiritual immaturity within the Corinthian Church. These believers in Corinth should have long since grown out of the "infant" stage and been maturing in their faith. Instead, they were still acting like "infants," so, Paul had to *feed* them (teach them) *with milk and not with solid food*—meaning that he had to continue to give them the basics of the faith instead of being able to teach them deeper truths.[233]

I'll never forget, this little old lady we had at our church once named Beverly. Beverly had a doctorate in Hebrew studies from the 1940s, but she came to watch one of my first sermons back at our old building, "Covenants". I remember going through all five of God's covenants in one sermon! Beverly proclaimed, "You don't feed them meat right away, give them some milk first." She was probably right, now that I look back on it, so I apologize to those that may have been overwhelmed by that sermon. But she was referring to Paul's advice here to the church in Corinth.

Another thought-provoking observation in this chapter of Corinthians is that Paul tells the Corinthians not to say that they belong to Apollos, or other leaders in the church, or even Paul himself. Today, televangelists and other popular Christian leaders, tend to bring glory to themselves, as opposed to bringing glory to God by taking credit for God's work in other people's lives.

One interesting fact about Martin Luther is that he was opposed to naming a denomination after himself:

> *I ask that my name be left silent and people not call themselves Lutheran, but rather Christians. Who is Luther? The doctrine is not mine. I have been crucified for no one. St. Paul in 1 Cor. 3:4-5 would not suffer that the Christians should call themselves of Paul or of Peter, but Christian. How should I, a poor stinking bag of worms, become so that the children of Christ are named with my unholy name? It should not be dear friends. Let us extinguish all factious names and be called Christians whose doctrine we have. The pope's men rightly have a factious name because they are not satisfied with the doctrine and name of Christ and want to be with the pope, who is their master. I have not been*

---

[233] Barton and Osborne, *1 & 2 Corinthians: Life Application Bible Commentary*, 48.

*and will not be a master. Along with the church I have the one general teaching of Christ who alone is our master. Matt. 23:8.*[234]

Therefore, it's truly best to not let the left hand know what the right hand is doing.[235]

Plants are very important. They give us food so that we can survive. Long before the days of processed foods, and garage freezers that could store food for months, there was a time when people depended upon God to grow plants so that they might produce fruits and vegetables after the sowing season. They depended upon God to bring reaping to their sowing; it truly was a matter of life and death.

We are still dependent upon God to provide all the elements that grow our plants (sunshine, soil, water), yet now, we like to give all of the credit to science. My cherished Spiritual Formation Professor, Dr. Calvin Blom always spoke about growing our roots deeper. The reason we feel distant from God or become susceptible to the world's sins is that we haven't let our roots grow deep into God's soil. We need to spend time in prayer, solitude, and the Word to help grow our roots profoundly. Jesus once said:

> *Hear then the parable of the sower. When anyone hears the word of the kingdom and does not understand it, the evil one comes and snatches away what has been sown in his heart. This is the one on whom seed was sown beside the road. The one on whom seed was sown on the rocky places, this is the man who hears the word and immediately receives it with joy; yet he has no firm root in himself, but is only temporary, and when affliction or persecution arises because of the word, immediately he falls away. And the one on whom seed was sown among the thorns, this is the man who hears the word, and the worry of the world and the deceitfulness of wealth choke the word, and it becomes unfruitful. And the one on whom seed was sown on the good soil, this is the man who hears the word and understands it; who indeed bears fruit and brings forth, some a hundredfold, some sixty, and some thirty.*[236]

You see, God does the sowing in our hearts, but if we don't let the Spirit discern it for us, the Evil One takes the message away.

---

[234] Luther, "Admonition Against Insurrection," 1522.
[235] Matt. 6:3 (Emphasis mine).
[236] Matt. 13:18-23 (NASB).

The second type of person is one who sows seeds on rocky places. He hears what God is saying and is joyous about the news, yet he is not rooted in his walk with Christ, so he gives into worldly temptations. The third type of person is one who hears the Word, but the thorns of the world, like anxiety, wealth, and deceit, pollute his heart and chokes God's words so that he bears no fruit.

Lastly, the man whom has a rooted relationship with Christ; the good soil, this is the one who not only understands what God tells him but also bears good fruit, the best fruit, which is the first fruits of the harvest, so that he bears fruit for others to see, a hundredfold. The purpose of every seed is to reproduce its own kind. Each seed has the potential to grow into a new, fully mature plant. In the same way, God is reproducing His "own kind" through man. As His "first fruits," God gave us the "seed" of His Spirit, with the potential to become like Him—having perfect character.

To grow in Christ requires two things: God growing us through the Holy Spirit, and our active participation in that growth. We must be actively engaged in sanctification. As mentioned in a previous chapter, there are three parts to salvation. 1) I was saved from the eternal consequences of sin at the cross. 2) I am being saved now by being sanctified or "set apart" and transformed to Christ's likeness. 3) And, I will be saved from the sin on this earth when Christ returns. This is how God will grow us into full maturity in Jesus Christ.

In my graduate studies at Multnomah University, I had to take four semesters of Greek. Those of you who have taken Greek know how much work goes into learning the language. Yet, there is also a great incentive in being able to read God's New Testament words in their original language. During my last semester of Greek, (Greek Exegesis) our final paper involved choosing a passage from Paul's epistle to the Ephesians and deducting principles and meaning from the passage in the original language. My paper ended up being twenty pages long, so I won't bore you with all the details here, but I would like to share with you some of the powerful insights that the Holy Spirit revealed to me during my study of unity in the body of Christ from Ephesians chapter four verses one through seven and the application to us in verses eight through sixteen, as they directly pertain to achieving maturity as Christ's church; both individually, and corporately. I apologize in advance if this section reads rather "heady," however it was a document that I spent well over eighty hours researching and writing. I've included my annotated footnotes for reference.

There are two primary theological themes in Ephesians that tie in with the rest of the New Testament Epistles and even tie in with the entire Bible. 1) Christ has reconciled all of creation unto Himself and to God, and 2) Christ has united people from all nations to Himself and one another in His church. These great deeds were accomplished by faith alone through God's grace.

Ephesians closely parallels Colossians in developing the metaphor of Christ as the head of the body, the church, thus stressing the churchly unity of Gentile and Jewish believers. The passage we're looking at from Ephesians 4:1-7, speaks of unity in the body and Spirit of Christ. We (the Church) have been called to be unified because God, Himself is unified. God is unified within the Godhead (God the Father, God the Son, God the Holy Spirit), or what is doctrinally known as "The Trinity." Genesis 1:26 says,

*Let us make mankind in our image, in our likeness, so that they may rule over the fish in the sea and the birds in the sky, over the livestock and all the wild animals, and over all the creatures that move along the ground.* [237]

The prophet Zechariah spoke for God when He said: "And the Lord will be king over all the earth. On that day the Lord will be one and his name one" (Zech. 14:9, ESV). Not that, on the last day, the Lord will become the Trinity, but rather, that on the last day, everyone will acknowledge one God, Yahweh, the God of Abraham, Isaac, and Jacob.[238]

---

[237] See Gen. 1:26 (NIV). Note the author's use of 1st person *plural* pronouns to refer to one God.

[238] 14:1–21 Jerusalem Divides the Spoil: Feast of Booths Kept. In Zechariah 14:1–5 the prophet described the events associated with the second coming of the Messiah at the end of the campaign of Armageddon (Rev. 16:16). Just before the Messiah's return, the unbelieving Gentile nations will gather at Jerusalem to besiege and destroy the city (Zech. 12:2). Christ's return to Jerusalem will turn what seems an unavoidable defeat into victory (14:4–9). Christ will return to the Mount of Olives, the very mountain from which he ascended (Acts 1:10–11). The splitting of the Mount of Olives will provide a way of escape for the besieged and defeated people in Jerusalem. The site of "Azal" (Zech. 14:5) has not been identified but must be somewhere in the desert east of Jerusalem. According to Josephus, the "earthquake" (14:5) occurred when Uzziah went into the temple to offer incense (cf. 2 Chron. 26:16–21). **king over all...earth**—Is 54:5 implies that this is to be the consequence of Israel being again recognized by God as His own people (Da 2:44; Rev 11:15). **One Lord...name one**— Not that He is not so already, but He shall then be *recognized by all unanimously* as "One." Now there are "gods many and lords many." Then Jehovah alone shall be worshipped. The *manifestation* of the unity of the Godhead shall be simultaneous with that of the unity of the

The early church struggled with idolatry, false prophets, and division. And now I'd like to turn to a verse by verse explanation to see how Paul addresses these issues with the church in Ephesus.[239]

*I Paul, a prisoner of the Lord strongly urges you to live a life worthy of the calling in which you have been called.*[240]

Paul repeats this characterization from Ephesians chapter 3:1c of being a "Prisoner of the Lord." [241] Paul initiates his exhortation with a reference to his own imprisonment. Paul not only refers to himself as a prisoner

---

Church. Believers are one in spirit already, even as God is one (Eph 4:3–6). But externally there are sad divisions. Not until these disappear, shall God reveal fully His unity to the world (Jn 17:21, 23). Then shall there be "a pure language, that all may call upon the name of the Lord with one consent" (Zep 3:9). The Son too shall at last give up His mediatorial kingdom to the Father, when the purposes for which it was established shall have been accomplished, "that God may be all in all" (1 Co 15:24). See Robert B. Hughes and J. Carl Laney, *Tyndale Concise Bible Commentary*, The Tyndale Reference Library (Wheaton, IL: Tyndale House Publishers, 2001), 381–382.

[239] Chapter two of Ephesians introduces oneness in Christ between the uncircumcision (Gentiles) and the circumcision (Jews). Both ethnic groups are now fellow citizens with the saints and members of the household of God. Paul begins chapter three with a cause statement: Τούτου χάριν "On account of this/For this reason." Then, Paul reveals the mystery of the Gospel which is that the Gentiles are fellow heirs, members of the same body, and partakers of the promise (*that was given to the Jews during the Abrahamic Covenant*) in Christ Jesus. There is a literary transition in Ephesians 3:14-21, in which Paul again begins with a cause statement: Τούτου χάριν "On account of this/For this reason." And then prays for Spiritual strength. Paul begins with another principle statement in chapter five (οὖν), and transitions into talking about walking in love and avoiding sexual immorality. Paul ends chapter five talking about wives and husbands in regard to submission and how loving our wives relates to Christ loving the church. Lastly, Paul talks about bondservants, the whole armor of God in spiritual battle, and final greetings. Paul remains focused on the church throughout this epistle, noting that Christ has reconciled all creation to Himself and to God, and that Christ has united people from all nations to Himself and to one another as part of His church. These deeds were accomplished by faith alone through God's grace. See Eph. 2-6/ ESV Study Bible (Wheaton: Crossway, 2008), 2250-2258.

[240] Eph. 4:1 (Emphasis mine).

[241] Overspecification—The description of individuals or ideas that is more specific than required to identify the intended referent. This extra information is often 'thematically-loaded', connected to the theme of the context in some way. The overspecification prompts the reader conceptualize the referent in a specific way. See the *Introduction* for further discussion on Overspecification. See Steven E. Runge, *The Lexham Discourse Greek New Testament: Glossary* (Lexham Press, 2008), 18.

in chapter three of this epistle but also in his epistle on behalf of the slave Philemon.[242] In many ways, we also give up certain freedoms for our faith.

Christians are obligated/strongly urged to live their lives in a way that is honoring to God.[243] The Greek word used here is Παρακαλῶ (I beg/I implore). Paul is literally begging the Ephesians to live a life in which they have been called; a godly life that is worthy of Christ's death on the cross for them.[244]

You can just imagine Paul's genuine love for the Christians in Ephesus. He's concerned with their behavior because it's dishonoring God and creating division in the church. Can you think of believers who behave this way today?

The adverb, "worthily" is not to be confused with the adjective "worthy." Paul is calling us to live our lives according to God's magnificent plan in chapter one; "that we might know the hope to which he has called us, that _we are_ the riches of his glorious inheritance in the saints, and that there is immeasurable greatness of his power towards us who believe."[245]

As Christians, we should be set apart from the indulgences of the world, the desires of the flesh, and the influences of the devil. This calling also involves the fulfillment of God's purpose to unite Jews and Gentiles in the church.[246]

*A life of humility and gentleness; a life of patience that bears with one another in love.*[247]

"Walking worthily" is explained by three qualities, the first being humility or lowliness. In common use, the word carries the sense of servility or weakness, but in the Bible, it carries the sense of divine recognition and

---

[242] Liefeld, Ephesians, vol. 10, *The IVP New Testament Commentary*, Eph 4:1-17.

[243] Appeal — The speaker is presenting the content of a request. See Mark Keaton, *The Lexham Propositional Outlines Glossary* (Bellingham, WA: Lexham Press, 2014), 25.

[244] Παρακαλῶ can also mean, "to urge strongly, *appeal to, urge, exhort, encourage*." See William Arndt, Frederick W. Danker, and Walter Bauer, *A Greek-English Lexicon of the New Testament and Other Early Christian Literature* (Chicago: University of Chicago Press, 2000), 765.

[245] Ephesians 1:18-19 (emphasis, mine).

[246] See Ephesians chapters 2-3.

[247] Eph. 4:2 (Emphasis mine).

submission. Similarly, we use the terms gentleness or meekness in a some-what shameful way, but the Greek word during biblical times for gentleness or "meekness" is best translated as "strength under pressure" or "strength under control."[248]

God calls us to be patient with one another. How are we doing when it comes to patience? I had a professor once that said he does well in every area of his Christian life, except for patience when he's driving. Perhaps some of you can relate?

The participial clause of "bearing with one another" elaborates upon the humility, gentleness, and patience in which we are *to live* worthily of our

---

[248] *The meek* (οἱ πραεῖς). Another word which, though never used in a bad sense, Christianity has lifted to a higher plane, and made the symbol of a higher good. Its primary meaning is *mild, gentle.* It was applied to inanimate things, as light, wind, sound, sickness. It was used of a horse; *gentle.* As a human attribute, Aristotle defines it as *the mean between stubborn anger and that.* Negativeness *of character which is incapable of even righteous indignation:* according to which it is tantamount to *equanimity.* Plato opposes it to fierceness or cruelty and uses it of humanity to the condemned; but also, of the conciliatory demeanor of a demagogue seeking popularity and power. Pindar applies it to a king, *mild* or *kind* to the citizens, and Herodotus uses it as opposed to anger. These pre-Christian meanings of the word exhibit two general characteristics. 1. They express *outward conduct* merely. 2. They contemplate relations to *men only.* **The Christian word, on the contrary, describes an *inward* quality, and that as related primarily to *God.* The *equanimity, mildness, kindness,* represented by the classical word, are founded in self-control or in natural disposition.** The Christian *meekness* is based on *humility,* which is not a natural quality but an outgrowth of a renewed nature. To the pagan the word often implied *condescension,* to the Christian it implies *submission.* The Christian quality in its manifestation, reveals all that was best in the heathen virtue—mildness, gentleness, equanimity—but these manifestations toward men are emphasized as outgrowths of a spiritual relation to God. The *mildness* or *kindness* of Plato or Pindar imply no sense of inferiority in those who exhibit them; sometimes the contrary. Plato's demagogue is kindly from self-interest and as a means to tyranny. Pindar's king is condescendingly kind. The meekness of the Christian springs from a sense of the inferiority of the creature to the Creator, and especially of the *sinful* creature to the *holy* God. While, therefore, the pagan quality is redolent of *self-assertion,* the Christian quality carries the flavor of *self-abasement.* As toward God, therefore, meekness accepts his dealings without murmur or resistance as absolutely good and wise. As toward man, it accepts opposition, insult, and provocation, as God's permitted ministers of a chastening demanded by the infirmity and corruption of sin; while, under this sense of his own sinfulness, the meek bears patiently "the contradiction of sinners against himself," forgiving and restoring the erring in a spirit of meekness, considering himself, lest he also be tempted (see Gal. 6:1–5). The ideas of forgiveness and restoration nowhere attach to the classical word. They belong exclusively to Christian meekness, which thus shows itself allied to love. As ascribed by our Lord to himself, see on Matt. 11:29. Wyc. renders "Blessed be *mild* men. See Marvin Richardson Vincent, *Word Studies in the New Testament,* vol. 1 (New York: Charles Scribner's Sons, 1887), 37–38.

calling.[249] The phrase "bearing with one another" or "putting up with one another, as we might say, is rooted in love.[250] How many churches are divided today because we fail to bear with one another in love when it comes to differences in non-essential Christian doctrines? Quite a few, that I know of.

> *We should be eager (zealous) to keep the unity of the Spirit in a peaceful manner.*[251]

We should be excited to be unified in the Spirit. The infinitive "to keep" is powerful here. Notice, it does not say, "to accomplish." This is because Christ accomplished our unity on the cross; it's now our job *to keep* that unity in a peaceful manner.[252]

I've seen so many people separate or leave churches because of petty differences. As long as what is taught is not contrary to Christian orthodox doctrine, we can agree to disagree on types of music, or pictures on the walls, or how long a sermon should be, or what we should wear to church services, etc.

> *The body of Christ is one, just like there is one Spirit of God. We are called in the one hope of our calling.*[253]

The oneness of the body of Christ has already been explained by Paul in chapters two and three. We just looked at the various manners in which we should be living according to our calling, and now we will get into the doctrines that are basic to Christian unity, here in verses four through six.

Paul uses a conjunction "and" to connect one body and one Spirit. This is because Paul is demonstrating that the body and Spirit are combined to make one unit. Paul uses this same analogy in his first letter to the Corinthians. [254]

---

[249] ἀνεχόμενοι modifies the verb περιπατῆσαι from chapter four verse one. See Albert L. Lukaszewski and Mark Dubis, *The Lexham Syntactic Greek New Testament: Expansions and Annotations* (Logos Bible Software, 2009), Eph. 4.

[250] Liefeld, Ephesians, vol. 10, *The IVP New Testament Commentary Series*, Eph 4:1-17.

[251] Eph. 4:3 (Emphasis mine).

[252] See Eph. 2:11-22, Gal. 3:28, 1 Cor. 12:5-6, Col. 3:14.

[253] Eph. 4:4 (Emphasis mine).

[254] See 1 Cor. 12:12-13.

It's interesting how many times Paul uses the adjective "one" in a parallel manner in this passage. There are actually seven occurrences between verses four and six.[255] Paul is emphasizing unity here intentionally; he wants us to be unified as brothers and sisters in Christ.

*The one hope in which we have been called* refers back to chapter four verse one, which alludes to Ephesians chapter one verse eighteen, which refers to what is explained in Ephesians chapter one verses three through fourteen. This includes "the redemption of those who are God's possession—to the praise of His glory" (1:14).[256]

So, our hope is not just what we shall experience and enjoy, but the joy and praise that shall come *to Christ* through those he has redeemed.[257] Most scholars take the prepositional phrase, "in the hope of your calling" to be a preposition of location, meaning that "in" expresses the ethical domain or element in which the calling took place; however, there is an argument that this is a preposition of "means" in which it functions as an instrumental preposition as in Galatians 1:6, the point being that the calling came "by" means of one hope. viz., that of the Messianic salvation.[258]

Notice, that the Greek word "also" is translated not as a conjunction, as "kai" would normally be translated, but rather, as an adverb. This is because Paul is creating a connection between two things.[259] Paul is adding

---

[255] εἷς, μία, ἕν, gen. ἑνός, μιᾶς, ἑνός a numerical term, 'one' (Hom.+)
① a single pers. or thing, with focus on quantitative aspect, *one*
ⓐ in contrast to more than one. See William Arndt, Frederick W. Danker, and Walter Bauer, *A Greek-English Lexicon of the New Testament and Other Early Christian Literature* (Chicago: University of Chicago Press, 2000), 565.
[256] Liefeld, Ephesians, vol. 10, *The IVP New Testament Commentary Series*, Eph 4:1-17.
[257] Ibid.
[258] "Ephesians 4," Expositor's Greek Testament, Bible Hub, accessed February 25, 2020, https://biblehub.com/commentaries/expositors/ephesians/4.htm.
[259] Thematic Addition—The use of καὶ as an adverb (instead of as a conjunction) to create a connection between two things, essentially 'adding' the current element to some preceding parallel element. Thematic addition is generally translated in English using 'also' or 'too'. Thematic addition can also be used to indicate confirmation of something, which is generally translated in English using 'even'. Cf. Levinsohn (2000:100). See the *Introduction* for further discussion on Thematic Addition. See Steven E. Runge, *The Lexham Discourse Greek New Testament: Glossary* (Lexham Press, 2008), 85.

this current statement to the previous statement in verse one, in which we are to act worthily of our calling. So, not only are we called to act worthily, but we are *also* called in the one hope.

What is the one hope to which we are called? Again, it goes all the way back to chapter one. It is that we experience and enjoy the riches of his glorious inheritance in the saints, *who have been redeemed*, and the immeasurable greatness of his power towards us who believe.[260]

*There is one Lord, one faith, and one baptism.*[261]

These are all parallel cardinal adjectives that are listed in bullets.[262] We must remember that there is only <u>one</u> Lord. This is the key to Christianity. Paul is demonstrating unity and exclusivity in the same verse.[263] There is one faith or "trust" in our belief in Christ Jesus, and there is also one baptism into Christ. One baptism does not refer to the mode of baptism, but rather that there is only one person into which Christian believers can be baptized; expressing their celebration of a heart transformation.[264]

*There is one God of all of us; He is over all of us, through all of us, and inside of all of us.*[265]

The argument for unity now reaches its climax in the nature of God. The threefold structure of the body, Spirit, calling; and the Lord, faith, and baptism is now used to heighten the "oneness" of God. He is transcendent, pervasive, and immanent.[266]

God is over all of us, meaning that we subordinate to Him. [267] God is the God and Father of everyone, whether you believe in Him or not. The

---

[260] See Ephesians 1:18-19.

[261] Eph. 4:5 (Emphasis mine).

[262] Bullet—A part of a clause that has been placed on its own line to attract attention to parallelism, a list, or a point-counterpoint set. The bullet is a dependent component of another clause. See Steven E. Runge, *The Lexham Discourse Greek New Testament: Glossary* (Lexham Press, 2008), 11.

[263] See Duet. 6:4

[264] Liefeld, Ephesians, vol. 10, *The IVP New Testament Commentary Series*, Eph 4:1-17.

[265] Eph. 4:6 (Emphasis mine).

[266] Liefeld, Ephesians, vol. 10, *The IVP New Testament Commentary Series*, Eph 4:1-17.

[267] Characterization — The speaker is describing someone or something in further detail. See Mark Keaton, *The Lexham Propositional Outlines Glossary* (Bellingham, WA: Lexham Press,

beauty of Christianity is that it doesn't matter where you are from, what gender you are, what you've done in your past, or what ethnicity or socio-economic status that you represent. We are all equal members of one family of Christ.

Paul, by stating that God is over all, through all, and in all may refer back to the fulness of the church with its combined elements of Jew and Gentile.[268] We've looked at the purpose of Paul's exhortation in chapter four, and now we will turn to the application in verses seven through sixteen, which refers to how we are to achieve unity as a church body.

> *But to each one of us grace was given according to the measure of Christ's gift.*[269]

The adversative conjunction used here is an important one. In saying "but," Paul is arguing that unity is very different than uniformity.[270] We are all united in the same faith and the one hope of Christ, *but* we have different gifts that we collectively use to help mature the Church.[271]

Something else happening in verse seven is that Paul switches pronouns from 2nd person plural "you all" to 1st person plural "we/us/our." Did you notice that? So, not only is Paul moving from unity to individuality as a theme, but he also moves grammatically from 2nd person plural in verses one through three to third person in verses four through six, and then includes himself in verse seven. And as we will see, he will include himself in verses thirteen, fourteen, and fifteen as well.[272]

---

2014), 13.

[268] Liefeld, Ephesians, vol. 10, *The IVP New Testament Commentary Series*, Eph 4:1-17.

[269] Eph 4:7 (NASB).

[270] Explanation **Experience** — The speaker is describing someone, or something undergoing or being affected by an action or event. See Mark Keaton, *The Lexham Propositional Outlines Glossary* (Bellingham, WA: Lexham Press, 2014), 28.

[271] de **"but"** - but, and. Possibly adversative as Paul moves from unity to diversity, although as a new subject it may be intended as a transitional connective marking a step in the argument and therefore not translated. Paul now qualifies the unity possessed of believers by identifying the diversity that exists within unity. Unity does not mean uniformity. See Daniel Wallace, *Greek Grammar: Beyond the Basics* (Grand Rapids: Zondervan, 1996), 657.

[272] Liefeld, Ephesians, vol. 10, *The IVP New Testament Commentary Series*, Eph 4:1-17.

> *When He ascended on high, He led captive a host of captives, And He gave gifts to men. (Now this expression, 'He ascended,' what does it mean except that He also had descended into the lower parts of the earth? He who descended is Himself also He who ascended far above all the heavens, so that He might fill all things.)[273]*

Paul, being the Pharisee of Pharisees, certainly knew his Old Testament. Remember, the New Testament was still being written, and more than likely, Paul, himself did not realize that what he was writing would one day be included in God's Holy Bible as we know it today.

Here, Paul is referencing Psalm 68:18 to explain that Jesus is the one that the Psalmist is referring to who gave gifts to men. The New Testament writers frequently quoted verses, used terminology, and alluded to ideas from Old Testament passages. Paul saw significance in connecting this psalm with God's distribution of gifts among Christian believers.[274]

Paul uses an interpretive device that may have resonated better with his audience than it does with us today.[275] There are two views on how to interpret this passage. The first view is that the emphasis here is on the ascent, rather than the descent and that more than likely, Paul is referring to Christ's descent prior to His ascent. Meaning that before Christ's incarnation, He descended from Heaven and then returned back there after His resurrection.[276]

---

[274] Eph 4:8–10 (NASB).

[274] Liefeld, Ephesians, vol. 10, *The IVP New Testament Commentary Series*, Eph 4:1-17.

[275] Interpretation — The speaker is assigning a specific meaning to another statement or event. See Mark Keaton, *The Lexham Propositional Outlines Glossary* (Bellingham, WA: Lexham Press, 2014), 25.

[276] The Old Testament text speaks of Yahweh's ascent; the text here refers to Christ's. In view of that exaltation, it was natural for the reader to apply the imagery of the psalm to Christ. Paul's contribution to New Testament Christology through his teaching about the descent and subsequent ascent of Christ (especially Phil 2:6–11, building on Jesus' own teaching in Jn 3:13; 6:62) is reflected in this passage (vv. 9–10).* The emphasis is clearly on the ascent, rather than the descent, with an expansive phrase, *higher than all the heavens* and the subsequent purpose clause, *in order to fill the whole universe.* The idea of filling the universe conforms to 1:23 and calls to mind the idea of the filling in other contexts: Ephesians 3:19; 5:18; and Colossians 1:9, 25; 2:10. See Walter L. Liefeld, *Ephesians*, vol. 10, The IVP New Testament Commentary Series (Downers Grove, IL: InterVarsity Press, 1997), Eph 4:8. This explanation does seem to represent what Jesus, Himself says according to John's gospel account. See also: John 3:13; 6:62: "No one has ever gone into heaven except the one who

The other popular view is that the descension refers to Christ's burial following His crucifixion because of the phrase "the lower parts of the earth." This would be in contrast to "far above all the heavens." The Apostle's Creed reflects the idea that Christ descended into "hell" to witness to both believers and unbelievers that He indeed was the prophesied Messiah.[277] "He might fill all things" harkens back to Ephesians chapter three verse nineteen, in which we might be filled with all the fullness of God by knowing the love of Christ.[278]

> *And He gave some as apostles, and some as prophets, and some as evangelists, and some as pastors and teachers, for the equipping of the saints for the work of service, to the building up of the body of Christ; until we all attain to the unity of the faith, and of the knowledge of the Son of God, to a mature man, to the measure of the stature which belongs to the fullness of Christ.[279]*

---

came from heaven—the Son of Man." (NIV) "Then what if you see the Son of Man ascend to where he was before!" (NIV). **When he ascended**—GOD is meant in the Psalm, represented by the ark, which was being brought up to Zion in triumph by David, after that "the Lord had given him rest roundabout from all his enemies" (2 Sa 6:1–7:1; 1 Ch 15:1–29). Paul quotes it of CHRIST ascending to heaven, who is therefore GOD. See Robert Jamieson, A. R. Fausset, and David Brown, *Commentary Critical and Explanatory on the Whole Bible*, vol. 2 (Oak Harbor, WA: Logos Research Systems, Inc., 1997), 350.

[277] lower parts of the earth—The antithesis or contrast to "far above all heavens," is the argument of Alford and others, to show that this phrase means more than simply the *earth,* namely, the regions *beneath* it, even as He ascended not merely to the visible heavens, but "far above" them. Moreover, His design "that He might fill *all* things" (Eph 4:10, *Greek,* "the whole universe of things") may imply the same. But see on Eph 4:10 on those words. Also, the leading "captive" of the "captive hand" ("captivity") of satanic powers, may imply that the warfare reached to *their habitation itself* (Ps 63:9). Christ, as Lord of all, took possession first of the earth the unseen world beneath it (some conjecture that the region of the lost is in the central parts of our globe), then of heaven (Ac 2:27, 28). However, all we *surely* know is, that His soul at death descended to Hades, that is, underwent the ordinary condition of departed spirits of men. The leading captive of satanic powers here, is not said to be at His descent, but *at His ascension;* so that no argument can be drawn from it for a descent to the abodes of Satan. Ac 2:27, 28, and Ro 10:7, favor the view of the reference being simply to His descent to Hades. So, Pearson in *Exposition of the Creed* (Php 2:10). See Robert Jamieson, A. R. Fausset, and David Brown, *Commentary Critical and Explanatory on the Whole Bible*, vol. 2 (Oak Harbor, WA: Logos Research Systems, Inc., 1997), 350.

[278] "And to know the love of Christ that surpasses knowledge, that you may be filled with all the fullness of God" See Ephesians 3:19 (ESV).

[279] Eph 4:11–13 (NASB).

What are these measured gifts that Christ gave to the church through God's grace? Christ's "gifts to men" is referring directly back to verses seven and eight. The functional gifts of apostles, prophets, evangelists, pastors, and teachers were all given to the church for the general purposes explained in verses twelve and thirteen, and for the specific purpose found in the subordinate clause of verse fourteen.[280]

According to verse thirteen, these ministries will be here until we attain to the unity of faith and the knowledge of the son of God in *maturity* according to Christ's standards.[281] Which, I argue will be when Christ/the "perfect" comes back.[282]

> *So that, we are no longer to be children, tossed here and there by waves and carried about by every wind of doctrine, by the trickery of men, by craftiness in deceitful scheming; but speaking the truth in love, we are to grow up in all aspects*

---

[280] I've chosen not to expand upon the issue of whether or not verse 11 describes functions or offices of the ministry. IVP explains this controversy in further detail: Recently the issue of whether verse 11 describes functions or offices of ministry has received much attention. One reason this is a difficult issue to resolve is that some of the epistles emphasize function (notably 1 Cor) whereas others, specifically the Pastorals, are thought to embody the idea that only certain designated persons carry on the major ministries of the church. It has been said that the Corinthian atmosphere is charismatic, but not that of the Pastorals. The differences are not as marked as sometimes thought. First Corinthians 12:27–31 lists specific classes of people doing ministry, and conversely 1 Timothy speaks of "gift" and a "prophetic message" in the very passage that used to be (mistakenly) thought of as portraying ordination (4:14). If pastors and teachers are to be thought of as offices, one has to demonstrate first that there were "offices" in the New Testament church. There is no Greek word in the New Testament corresponding to "office." The term did occur in the King James Version, but without warrant in the Greek text. See Walter L. Liefeld, Ephesians, vol. 10, *The IVP New Testament Commentary Series* (Downers Grove, IL: InterVarsity Press, 1997), Eph. 4:1-17.
[281] Ultimate — The speaker is stating information relevant to the final period of some span of time. See Mark Keaton, *The Lexham Propositional Outlines Glossary* (Bellingham, WA: Lexham Press, 2014), 89.
[282] Paul speaks of the spiritual gifts remaining in part until "the perfect" returns in 1 Corinthians 13: 8-10. While some argue that "the perfect/completeness" refers to scriptural canon, this would not make sense in the context of Paul's culture. Paul would not have known that his letters would one day be published and canonized several hundred years later. So, the most likely interpretation is that "the perfect" is referring to Jesus' return. In the Ephesians passage, maturity is defined as "attaining to the whole measure of the fullness of Christ." Such a state will obviously not exist until Christ's second coming. It would appear that the same perspective was developed in this passage to the Corinthians. See "What does 'when the perfect comes' mean in 1 Corinthians 13:9-10?," Bible.org, January 1, 2001, https://bible.org/question/what-does-"when-perfect-comes"-mean-1-corinthians-139-10.

*into Him who is the head, even Christ, from whom the whole body, being fitted and held together by what every joint supply according to the proper working of each individual part, causes the growth of the body for the building up of itself in love.*[283]

The subordinate clause, "ina" found at the beginning of verse fourteen gives us the answer to the question, "Why does Christ give us the gifts of apostles, evangelists, prophets, pastors, and teachers?" These gifts are given to the church so that we can be unified in maturity, free from teaching in deceit and cunning, and all other divisive sins that block us from the truth of relating to Christ and each other; that we may know the full knowledge of Christ and grow up in Him in love.

This is still a goal we are working towards. As you can see in the Christian community, we are all *not* united in the maturity of Christ. We are *not* free from deceit and cunning. Sadly, in some churches, Christ is not even the head! The pastor is. Paul ends with a continuing thought from verse fifteen[284] with the emphasis being on love as a means to achieve this goal.

We've seen how Paul wishes for us to be unified, and what gifts are provided for the church to achieve that goal. Now I'd like to share with you a story in which I and a good friend and pastor used our spiritual gifts together to help a believer mature in her faith.

About a year ago, I woke up in the middle of the night to my phone illuminating next to my bed. I wasn't sure who it was, but it turned out to be a Facebook notification from someone on my five thousand member friends list. So, after scrolling through Facebook for several minutes, because now I couldn't sleep, I came across a posting from a woman stating that she's literally taking full bottles of prescription pills and ending her life, in real-time. I looked through people's comments and she wasn't responding to anyone, so I reached out to her on private messenger and she responded to me. I spent the next four hours telling her that Satan is the one convincing her that nobody loves her, and that Jesus Christ will always love

---

[283] Eph 4:14–16 (NASB).

[284] Continuation — The speaker is picking up a train of thought that was interrupted; normally the interruption includes background information relevant to the main clause introduced in the Continuation. See Mark Keaton, *The Lexham Propositional Outlines Glossary* (Bellingham, WA: Lexham Press, 2014), 18.

her and that her life is precious to God, etc. I couldn't get her to reveal her address, but my intention was to get the paramedics over there to treat and evaluate her. Knowing that Michael wasn't far from the area of town she told me she was in, I asked for his help. Thankfully, she ended up being okay and getting out of a scary and abusive situation. Thanks be to God!

This is just one story of many that Michael and I, and any pastor that deals with pastoral care have to tell. I'm not up all night talking about theology with people, I'm giving life and death advice, and have to trust in the Holy Spirit 100% that what I am doing and saying is right.

In unity as part of Christ's gift of the fivefold ministry mentioned earlier in verse eleven, brother Michael, the evangelist, and I—the preacher-teacher—stood together, united against the demonic forces at play with this young lady. We prayed for her, prayed with her, and represented Christ's love to her. And her life was spared. I take no credit other than remaining obedient to God during this spiritual crisis in her life.

The application to us is that Christians must be unified because God, Himself is unified. Church unity and maturity can be achieved through Christ's gifts of the five-fold ministry until we have all reached full maturity. The aim of the Church is that her members should reach a stature that can be measured by the fullness of Christ. The aim of the Church is nothing less than to produce men and women who have in them the reflection of Jesus Christ, Himself.

There is one body. Christ is the head and the Church is the body. No brain can work through a body that is split into fragments. Unless there is a coordinated oneness in the body, the designs of the head are frustrated. The oneness of the Church is essential for the work of Christ. Unity does not mean uniformity, but the oneness needs to be founded on a common love of Christ and of every part of each other.

What we're really talking about here is separation; division, right? The opposite of unity is division. Satan loves to separate and divide us and has been doing so since the fall. His goal is not to get us on God's bad side, his goal is to entice us to sin to the point that it results in our eternal separation from the Father. And, this is why we need to separate ourselves from the world; from evil, and which is why we must be united as one body in Christ because we are better together. I'm better able to defeat the enemy because I have the help of all of you who are in agreement with core Christian doctrines and who are fighting the good fight alongside me.

Paul took a special interest in the unity within the body of believers, and he did not argue for an invisible bond but for a oneness that should characterize the visible body. He recognized unity in diversity and diversity in unity, and he amplified this approach (see 1 Cor. 12) with the appeal to love and the unifying bond (Ch. 13). The apostle looked upon unity as reality already in existence, but also as a reality yet to be attained. As we are "patient, bearing with one another in love," we are then eager "to keep the unity of the Spirit" (see Eph. 4:2-3). There exists this unity already, but it is the unity of the Spirit, and this feature relates to Paul's treatment of diversity in unity (see 1 Cor. 12, Eph. 4:7). One should thus expect "one Lord, one faith, one baptism" (see Eph. 4:5). That the real unity here described is not fully manifest in the church nor among the most ardent followers of Christ is quite clear, for Paul wrote of unity as something yet to be attained. There are varieties of gifts and offices for the building up of the body of Christ "until we all reach unity in the faith and in the knowledge of the Son of God." Then will come maturity, "the whole measure of the fullness of Christ" (see Eph. 4:13).[285]

No matter how good a sports player is, if he's on a team, he can't succeed against his opponents alone. Kobe Bryant, Michael Jordan, Shaquille O'Neal, all of these great basketball players had to depend upon their teammates to achieve their objective—to win the game. And, so do we in our objective to win in this game of life; to be unified in the fullness and maturity of Christ. Therefore, there is neither Jew nor Greek, there is neither slave nor free, there is no male and female, for you are all *one* in Christ Jesus.[286]

*Unity in the Church*

Our exegetical journey of Ephesians chapter four touched on Paul's goal for the church to be unified in the faith and knowledge of Jesus Christ and be mature according to Christ's standards. Now, I'd like to touch on corporate unity within the larger context of Christ's church.

---

[285] Leitch, *The Zondervan Encyclopedia of the Bible*, s.v. "Unity."
[286] Gal. 3:28 (ESV).

Several years ago, an elder at my church, and I went to an event in Reno, Nevada called, "One Cry." Their sole purpose is to promote prayer and unity among different believers in Christ; no different really than Paul did some two thousand years ago. Their website says, "One Cry is a diverse movement of Christians denominationally, geographically, generationally, and ethnically. However, we believe that all true Christian unity is in the gospel of Jesus Christ."[287]

In 1 Corinthians, the Apostle Paul notes that:

The eye cannot say to the hand, "I don't need you!" And the head cannot say to the feet, "I don't need you!" On the contrary, those parts of the body that seem to be weaker are indispensable, and the parts that we think are less honorable we treat with special honor. And the parts that are unpresentable are treated with special modesty, while our presentable parts need no special treatment. But God has put the body together, giving greater honor to the parts that lacked it, so that there should be no division in the body, but that its parts should have equal concern for each other. If one part suffers, every part suffers with it; if one part is honored, every part rejoices with it. Now you are the body of Christ, and each one of you is a part of it.[288]

Paul was pleading with the believers to *let there be real harmony* and for them to *be of one mind, united in thought and purpose*. To be perfectly united does not mean that Paul required everyone to be exactly the same. Instead, he wanted them to set aside their arguments and focus on what truly mattered—Jesus Christ as Lord and their mission to take the light of the gospel into a dark world. As Christians, we cross all boundaries of race, gender, socio-economic status, and intellect.

Christ Jesus sets individuals free from sin and death by making them alive through faith in Him (see Ephesians 2:1–10), but there is more to the story. Jesus saved individuals of all races and backgrounds to bring them into unity as His body; His church. There existed a huge gulf between Jews and Gentiles (non-Jews). God was going to bring these two distinct groups together by drawing believers in Christ from among the Jews *and* from

---

[287] "What is OneCry?" OneCry: A Nationwide Call for Spiritual Awakening, accessed May 13, 2020, https://onecry.com/about/.
[288] 1 Cor. 12:21-27 (NIV).

among the Gentiles. The Jews had the privilege of being God's chosen nation to whom He had given His covenant promises.[289]

One of the signs of His covenant was circumcision. God required circumcision as an act of obedience to Him, as a sign of belonging to His covenant people (because once circumcised, the man would be identified as a Jew forever), and as a symbol of "cutting off" the old life of sin, purifying one's heart, and dedicating oneself to God. More than any other practice, circumcision separated God's people from their Egyptian and Canaanite neighbors.[290] Circumcision was the Old Testament equivalent of being baptized, before water baptism came along.

Before the resurrection, we—*the Gentiles*—were separated from Christ, having had no expectation of a Messiah to save us. Gentiles were excluded from citizenship in Israel and could never fully partake of the spiritual privileges promised to Israel; God's chosen people. While Gentiles could become Jews after an extensive training period, followed by circumcision and baptism, the sense of "exclusion" was never fully removed. Gentiles could never truly be citizens of Israel.[291]

This is why God had hardened the hearts of the Jewish people. If He hadn't hardened their hearts, then the Jews would have never crucified Christ, and the Gentiles would have never had the opportunity to enter into the promised land.[292]

We are so blessed to have the advantage of being on the grace side of the Cross. Before the age of grace, was the age of the Law, in which no one could live up to, not even the chosen people of God, the Jews! Indeed, we are all in such a need of a savior.

Paul's letter to the Ephesians also speaks of breaking down the walls of hostility between the Jews and Gentiles.[293] Christ's sacrifice atoned for the sins of all kinds of people—Jews *and* Gentiles. Jews and Gentiles alike could be guilty of spiritual pride—Jews for thinking that their faith and tra-

---

[289] Barton and Comfort, *Ephesians*, 49.
[290] Ibid., 49–50.
[291] Ibid., 50.
[292] See Rom. 11:25.
[293] See Ephesians 2:14.

ditions elevated them above everyone else, Gentiles for trusting in their achievements, power, or position. Spiritual pride blinds us to our own faults and magnifies the faults of others. Be careful not to become proud of your salvation. Instead, humbly thank God for what He has done, and encourage others who might be struggling in their faith.[294]

Ephesians chapter two verse seventeen talks about peace. In addition to bringing peace to individuals and between people, Christ Himself *is our peace*. The prophet, Micah, wrote, "This One shall be peace,"[295] and Isaiah prophesied the coming of the Prince of Peace.[296] Unfortunately, this peace that Christ made between the two groups has not been the practical experience of Gentiles and Jews throughout history. The requirement for peace as defined here would be faith in Christ.[297]

The book of Hebrews tells us that Jesus belonged to the order of Melchizedek, who existed long before Levi or Aaron:

This Melchizedek was king of Salem and priest of God Most High. He met Abraham returning from the defeat of the kings and blessed him, and Abraham gave him a tenth of everything. First, the name Melchizedek means "king of righteousness"; then also, "king of Salem" means "king of peace." Without father or mother, without genealogy, without beginning of days or end of life, resembling the Son of God, he remains a priest forever... Now the law requires the descendants of Levi who become priests to collect a tenth from the people—that is, from their fellow Israelites—even though they also are descended from Abraham. This man, however, did not trace his descent from Levi, yet he collected a tenth from Abraham and blessed him who had the promises. And without doubt the lesser is blessed by the greater. In the one case, the tenth is collected by people who die; but in the other case, by him who is declared to be living. One might even say that Levi, who collects the tenth, paid the tenth through Abraham, because when Melchizedek met Abraham, Levi was still in the body of his ancestor.[298]

---

294 Barton and Comfort, *Ephesians*, 52.
295 Mic. 5:5 (NKJV).
296 See Isa. 9:6
297 Barton and Comfort, *Ephesians*, 52.
298 Heb. 7:1-10 (NIV).

Notice this passage says that Melchizedek means, "King of Righteousness, King of Peace." Jesus is known as the *Prince of Peace*. This passage reflects Jesus' earthly kingship through the line of David who established Israel's capital of Jerusalem which means, *City of Peace*. So, Jesus is not only the high priest through Melchizedek, but also Jesus is the King of Israel through David's line and the tribe of Judah. Peace is a requirement of unity.

Some have questioned, "Why did Jesus heal some people, but not others?" Jesus did not have consistency with healing because He was leading people into unity with the Lord. Sometimes Jesus would heal a Jew, sometimes a Gentile, sometimes a woman, sometimes a child, sometimes a Roman soldier, sometimes an enemy, and sometimes, a close friend. Subsequently, we cannot lead others towards glorification if we are divided by hate and prejudice ourselves. This is why it is so important to invest the time working on self-discovery and spiritual direction in our own lives before we ever take on the task of mentoring someone else.

Unity in God involves unity with each other. In her book, *Disunity*, Christina Cleveland points out:

> *As we've seen, the current depressing reality is that Christians often act as if the kingdom of God is supposed to look like the city they live in. In theory, we support the vision of a diverse, integrated and interdependent body of Christ, but we sure as heck don't want to venture outside of our homogenous churches to live the vision.* [299]

Cleveland is absolutely right. The issue is that we tend to rely more on our smaller cultural identities as opposed to the larger identity as members of Christ's body. When we come together, we ought not to see ourselves as threatening competitors, but as diverse fellow Christians. The Apostle Paul says that we are one body with many parts. We should embrace being the many parts of His body.

There is much power in being united with Christ. According to Francis Frangipane:

> *The benefits of Christ-centered unity are great. Just two or three united in a symphony of life drawn from Christ Himself escorts us to a spiritual realm*

---

[299] Cleveland, *Disunity in Christ*, 177.

*where, according to our Lord, every prayer has the potential to be answered. You see, oneness with God, with our spouse, and with other believers is not a fringe benefit: it is an ultimate goal in our quest for spiritual maturity.*[300]

Frangipane further notes that unity is essential today if we hope to see a great outpouring of the Spirit like that of Pentecost.[301]

When God asked Cain where his brother was at, He wasn't isolating His question to an Old Testament audience, but rather, He was essentially asking for us to be accountable to our brothers and sisters in Christ as well. We are still our brother's keepers. Today, He is still calling us to stop fighting and killing one another and instead, to unite in Christ so that we are stronger in the fight against evil. Therefore, first, make peace with your brother, then present your offering before the Lord (see Matt. 5:24).

Despite the fact that we are divided by denominations, we are all part of the same spiritual nation. We must step out of our comfort zones and embrace our brothers and sisters of different denominations with love. The ultimate way in which to demonstrate our union with Christ is to love Him by keeping His commandments.

We need to work at embracing our differences as long as they do not affect our core Christian beliefs. Diversity in the body of Christ is a beautiful thing. Frangipane once noted in his book on unity:

How strange that we smugly look upon the divisions in the Corinthian church. We boldly criticize their carnality. But why was it wrong in the 1st century to say, 'I am of Paul (or Apollos),' but permissible in these last days to say, 'I am of Luther…or Wesley…or the Baptists…or The Pentecostals.'[302]

I was very blessed to have an eclectic church background; from my time at the Lutheran Church to my experience with the Charismatics, to my current pleasure of serving at the First Church of God, Reno. One thing that I've always held to is that as believers, we don't have to be pigeonholed

---

[300] Frangipane, *Unity*, 5.
[301] Ibid.
[302] Ibid., 30. See also, section on *The Fully Mature Christian*.

into a certain denomination or belief system. Being Christ-centered in the way that we conduct ourselves is enough.

Division happens when we let Satan point out our differences instead of letting God elevate our similarities. We are all made in God's image, regardless if we are Jews or Gentiles. Egyptians, Jews, and Gentiles ethnically all trace back to Noah's sons: Ham, Shem, and Japheth. When I was taking Old Testament courses as an undergraduate at Multnomah University, I used to spend hours tracing the genealogies of these three groups.

Ham's descendants (the Canaanites) were cursed by his father Noah because Ham "saw him naked" and perhaps more disturbingly, did other things to him as well. Ham ends up being the patriarch of the Canaanite, Egyptian, and Philistine lines, who currently make up many of the Muslims in the Middle East today.

Shem is where we get the word, "Semitic" from, so Shem's descendants are the Hebrew line including Abraham, Isaac, and Jacob, Moses, King David, all of the prophets, all of the disciples, John the Baptist, Mary, Joseph, the Apostle Paul, and Jesus, Himself.

And lastly, Japheth is the father of the Gentile line, which is every one that is not Jewish or Egyptian; Japheth's line includes most of us. Though we were ethnically separated by Noah, we are all brought together by Christ.

Recently, I've been praying about the division and racial divide in our country, enhanced by the tragic death of George Floyd and other African Americans. I asked God what I could do as a small church pastor in Reno to help bring peace and unity back to our nation? He told me to contact every pastor in the area that I've ever interacted with and ask to set up a prayer event in the downtown Reno area to pray for social injustice, the safety of law enforcement, unity, and an end to the rioting and protests around our nation. To my amazement, and God's glory, more than one hundred pastors and faith leaders in our local area showed up with only two days' notice! I was so thankful that I listened to the Holy Spirit and was obedient to God's instruction in organizing the event. Sometimes we must step out in faith, outside of our comfort zones, to recognize what God is doing to unify His people.

Thanks to Jesus Christ's sacrifice on the cross, we all have one Holy Spirit that unites us to both, Christ, and each other. The kingdom of Heaven is at hand because Christ is the chief cornerstone and we are the bricks that make up the dwelling place of the Lord. Once we accept Jesus Christ into our hearts, the kingdom is no longer someplace far away in the sky, but rather, the kingdom is very close; it's right inside of us.

*Conclusion*

Chapter six is packed with spiritual and theological nuggets. Beginning with my own personal spiritual disciplines and practices that have helped me to grow in Christ through the power of the Holy Spirit, then transitioning into how we should be seed planters in the lives of every human being and allow God to grow us into mature Christians. We took an exegetical journey through Ephesians chapter four and the implications of being *one* in Christ as fully mature Christians, for God, Himself is one. To get there, we need the help of the five-fold ministry until *The Perfect* returns. And lastly, we explored unity within the Church.

All of these sections focused on corporate and individual responsibility to mature into Christlikeness. Mature churches have concentrated on these efforts and have reaped the benefits. Conversely, immature churches have chosen not to work together as one body and spirit, and have suffered great separation from the church community, and within their own denominations. Which church will you belong to?

# CHAPTER 7

## God's Dwelling Place

We are so important to God that He has chosen to give us a portion of Himself to keep with us wherever we go. No longer must we search for Him in the heavens, for He dwells inside of us at all times. God, who once dwelt in a temple made by human hands, became flesh at the incarnation and dwells among us now in the form of the Holy Spirit.

Perhaps, too often, we take for granted the datum that our bodies are actually temples of God. And, how many times have we fallen victim to cluttering up our temples with ungodly things? As I reflected on John chapter two and Jesus' cleansing of the temple, the Holy Spirit kept impressing upon me that this passage somehow connects to the cleansing of our bodies. I wasn't sure how to make the correlation completely until further prayer and study, but sure enough, I had a remarkable revelation: Jesus was cleansing the physical temple, but we must cleanse our bodies; our spiritual temples, because like a physical temple, our bodies are also Holy.

Have you ever had a smoothie from Jamba Juice? They pride themselves on using real fruit and organic ingredients. I can't remember every detail, but I do remember having my first Jamba Juice smoothie about fifteen years ago—or whenever the store in Reno had opened. A girl that I was dating at the time said, "Read what's written on the cup!" I turned the cup to the reverse side, and it said, "Your body is a temple; littering is strictly prohibited." I thought to myself, "Huh, that's pretty neat." I'm sure in the context of a smoothie company that promotes healthy, natural ingredients, they were trying to emphasize living a healthy lifestyle, but it got me thinking about how we treat our bodies. And actually, the Bible has quite a bit to say about our human bodies.

In writing to the believers in Corinth, the Apostle Paul once said, "Or do you not know that your body is a temple of the Holy Spirit within you, whom you have from God? You are not your own, for you were bought with a price. So, glorify God in your body."[303] Just three chapters prior, Paul tells us, "Do you not know that you are God's temple and that God's Spirit dwells in you? If anyone destroys God's temple, God will destroy him. For God's temple is holy, and you are that temple."[304]

Remarkably, the placement of Jesus cleansing the temple in John's gospel comes much sooner than in the synoptic gospels. Theologians argue that this was probably the case because John applied temple language to Jesus Christ. This constitutes the typological fulfillment of the Jerusalem sanctuary and its divine replacement.

Jesus displayed a supreme zeal for God's holiness and purity in His house. Verse seventeen of John chapter two is referring to Psalm 69:9: "For zeal for your house has consumed me, and the reproaches of those who reproach you have fallen on me."[305] We too must have this type of zeal for God's house. God's dwelling place was the Temple, now Jesus is the new raised up temple which dwells inside of us in the form of the Holy Spirit. We possess a bodily temple that often needs cleansing.

When I first started serving as the senior pastor of First Church of God Reno, almost six years ago now, I felt like there was some type of darkness dwelling in our old church building. I couldn't put my finger on it, but something didn't feel quite right when I was there by myself. So, as I do for my own house, I went over to the church one day and cleansed the property with olive oil. It definitely felt better, although admittedly, I probably needed to do it a few more times to purge all of the past sins of anger, lust, pride, and jealousy out. Yes, you read that correctly, Satan can even find his way into a church. So, not only should we cleanse our bodies after sinful behaviors, but we should cleanse our churches as well.

In an ungodly world, we must be the light that shines into the darkness. Much like Jesus clearing the temple was an example of a pure ray of light shining into a corrupt temple system, our light must continue to burn

---

[303] 1 Cor. 6:19-20 (ESV).
[304] 1 Cor. 3:16-17 (ESV).
[305] Ps. 69:9 (NIV).

brightly twenty-four hours a day, seven days a week. The Holy Spirit doesn't take a break, and neither should we. Work out your salvation with fear and trembling by cleansing the eternal temple within, and remember, your body is a temple; littering is strictly prohibited.

*Our True Identity in Christ*

Not much has changed in terms of how people perceive us, or how we perceive ourselves, since the Fall of mankind in Genesis chapter three. Sure, we now have cell phones, computers, and a host of other devices that make our lives easier, but our human characteristics, found within the Book of Proverbs, and contained within the identities of the mocker, the sluggard, the fool, and the wise man, remain relatively unchanged. Quite arguably, the wisest king who ever lived, King Solomon, who authored the Proverbs, eventually fell prey himself to the very folly that he writes about.

The Book of Proverbs is a collection of wise sayings and instructions for living a useful life. The collection forms part of a larger group of writings in the Bible known as wisdom literature. Proverbs are not unique to the Bible. There are several parallels to the wisdom literature of the ancient Near East; however, the biblical material *is* unique in its prerequisite of personal faith in a personal God. I'll begin with a look at the scoffer.

*A scoffer does not like to be reproved; he will not go to the wise.*[306]

The scoffer is full of pride yet lacks wisdom. The scoffer is someone we all know, someone we've all read about or heard, perhaps even someone we can personally identify with. In case you are unfamiliar with what a scoffer actually is, Proverbs 21 defines it for us: "An arrogant, haughty man who acts with arrogant pride."[307] A scoffer does not like his rebuke. Scoffers are characterized by their attitude, which prevents them from finding wisdom. In essence, the scoffer, at the time this was written, was one who scoffed not at belief, but at the Law.

I was on Facebook a few years ago and I ran across this evolutionist advertisement that supposed, "How the earth was formed." You can probably guess; they did not credit God with forming it. On the contrary, they

---

[306] Prov. 15:12 (ESV).
[307] Prov. 21:24 (ESV).

said it was a star that exploded and spits out atoms which then bonded to-gether and created the solar system and earth and all of the planets within the Milky Way. Of course, not being able to resist the temptation, I had to reply, "If your theory is true, then why is it that we don't see a new creation of planets with life on them (and entire new solar systems) each time a star explodes?" Not knowing exactly how often stars explode, I stated my ar-gument in faith.

Later, I looked up stars and supernova life cycles. In a NASA article I read, it said that the lifespan of a star is 10,000 years, but there are so many of them that one dies and explodes every 100 years or so on average. Therefore, I reasoned, that every 100 years we should see earth-like planets forming in outer space if their theory is true, right? You with me on this one? Since the scientific method requires duplication, then I was simply arguing that this could not be how the earth and life on it was formed. Of course, we as believers know that it was formed through God speaking it into existence!

You should have read the comments I received in response; hundreds of them. And, none that were even remotely respectful; many mocking Christianity, or religion in general. Scoffing at the very idea that I could be right, the comments got to the point where it wasn't worth me responding because it would just lead to a response from the evolutionists that would upset me even more. It was then that I realized that my goal was no longer speaking godly wisdom into unbelievers' lives, but rather, my goal was to try and prove that I was right; ironically, turning *me* into the scoffer that I so vehemently opposed to.

*The desire of the sluggard kills him, for his hands refuse to labor. All day long he craves and craves, but the righteous gives and does not hold back.*[308]

Those who are sluggish or *slothful* in their souls, refuse the pains neces-sary for spiritual blessings. Here, we have the miseries of the sluggard, whose *hands refuse to labor* in an honest calling, by which they might get an honest livelihood. They are as fit for labor as other men when business of-fers itself, to which they might lay their hands and apply their minds, but they will not make any effort to do so.

---

[308] Prov. 21:25-26 (ESV).

In contrast, we have an antithetical message at the end of verse twenty-six. The righteous and industrious have their desires satisfied and enjoy not only that satisfaction but the further satisfaction of doing good to others. The slothful are always craving and gaping to receive, *but the righteous* are always full and contriving to give; it is always more blessed to give than to receive.

Approximately twenty years ago, I was living with a woman in Las Vegas. Everything about our relationship and that particular location was toxic. Yet for some reason, I felt that I couldn't escape. We would break up, then get back together, then break up again, then get back together again. This cycle continued for five years; each time, I would uproot and make the drive from Reno to Las Vegas (these two cities are not as close as you might think. It's a good eight-and-a-half-hour drive between them), only to discover that I really wasn't happy at all. I was miserable with her, and I was miserable without her. Once, I had even boughten a large expanse of aspirin and was driving back to Las Vegas for the fifth time, about to ingest all of them, when by God's grace, the Lord told me to turn around. You see, I was craving my own desires instead of God's desires, and it was quite literally killing me.

What finally enabled my transition back to a healthier environment, was that I actively participated in God's plan for my life; I worked hard, participated in a small group with a great church, and didn't hold back in trying to model myself after God's righteousness. I concentrated and focused only on Him, and my relationship with Him. And, in return, I received His blessing of starting a business, working a second full-time job with benefits and health insurance, and even met my wife a year later. It always amazes me when people complain about their life, yet they refuse to take any steps to improve it. The Lord directs our steps, but *we still* must plan our way.

> *Like snow in summer or rain in harvest, so honor is not fitting for a fool. Like a sparrow in its flitting, like a swallow in its flying, a curse that is causeless does not alight. A whip for the horse, a bridle for the donkey, and a rod for the back of fools. Answer not a fool according to his folly, lest you be like him yourself. Answer a fool according to his folly, lest he be wise in his own eyes.[309]*

---

[309] Prov. 26:1-5 (ESV).

The fool says there is no God because he trusts in his own wisdom. The characteristics of a fool according to the Book of Proverbs are that the fool is unrighteous, unwise, not capable of obtaining wisdom, unrealistic, undisciplined, unreliable, and unteachable.

It is fascinating that Jesus speaks strongly against calling someone a fool in Matthew 5:22, yet does it Himself in Matthew 23:17. How can this be? Let's look at the biblical definition of a fool from Psalm 14:1: "The fool says in his heart, 'There is no God.' They are corrupt, they do abominable deeds; there is none who does good."[310] Here, we see that a fool is someone who says in their heart that there is no God. We cannot judge the hearts of men, only God can. Jesus knew their hearts because Jesus is God.

Sadly, we all know people that fall into this category, so we must continue to share the gospel message, so that one day, the unbeliever might proclaim, "There *is* a God, and we relate to Him through our faith in Jesus Christ."

*The fear of the Lord is the beginning of wisdom, and the knowledge of the Holy One is insight.*[311]

As you can see, I've saved the best for last; the Wiseman. Well, I'm sure you're asking yourself, who wouldn't want to be a wise man, or wise woman? I mean, wisdom is what we all want right? To be able to solve any problem, to understand complex things should be the desire of all of us. Wisdom is what we want to acquire as the years go on. But hear me well, our definition of wisdom and the biblical definition of wisdom are two very different things. A healthy fear of the Lord is what empowers us to make wise decisions.

It is not knowledge we should desire; the thing that tends to puff up, as Paul tells us, but rather, it is the fear of the Lord that we should be praying for. When we fear the consequences of our actions, we tend to make wiser choices. In the Old Testament, *the fear of the Lord* was used as a designation of true piety. It is a fear conjoined with love and hope and is therefore not a slavish dread, but rather filial reverence.

---

[310] Ps. 14:1 (ESV).
[311] Prov. 9:10 (ESV).

Doesn't it feel like very few people have a fear of the Lord nowadays? I promise you, when He spoke to Abraham, Isaac, Jacob, and Moses, there was fear, for they hid their very faces from Him. Not in fear of what God would do to them, but rather, in fear of what they had done to God.

Here's a surprise plot-twist for you. Our identity is not found in any of these characters. Our identity is found only in Jesus Christ! Bill Thrall once wrote that we see ourselves as sinners trying to become saints, but God sees us saints who sin.[312] If we label ourselves by certain characteristics that the world deems relevant, then we cannot live up to our full potential. Yet, if we identify ourselves as God already sees us, then we are obligated to live our lives that way. When we accepted Jesus Christ into our hearts, we became a new creation in Him. Our spiritual growth entails experientially growing into who we already are. We are no longer the sluggard, the wise man, the fool, or the mocker, we are born again; therefore, our identity is found in Jesus Christ, Himself!

*A Heart After God's Own Heart*

There's a reason that the Bible is so special. Not only is it a book about our creation, the fall, Jesus' life, His resurrection, our redemption, and our future glorification, but it has so many stories in it that we can read thousands of years later and still learn something from. It's a book of love, prophecy, a guidebook for our lives, a book of the revelation, a book of the life and passion of Jesus Christ, a book of good news, as well as a detailed historical document. It's all there; all in one book.

One famous biblical story that most people are familiar with, is that of King David and Bathsheba. This story relates to many of us in some way. No, I don't mean that we all have the spouses of our lovers murdered in battle, at least, I hope not; rather, I want to emphasize here how we tend to try and cover up our mistakes, or even add to them with more poor decisions. My treasured Old Testament History and Poetry professor called it, *The Sin Train.*

Much like a strong locomotive barreling down the tracks, once sin gains some momentum, it's fairly unstoppable. We've all seen those old westerns where the damsel in distress is tied to the train tracks by a villain,

---

[312] Thrall, *Communities of Grace*, quoted in Andrews, *The Kingdom Life*, 73.

and just before the train runs her over, a valiant hero unties her and they ride off into the sunset, gazing into one another's eyes as the credits begin to roll.

In real life, the analogy would be better compared to Satan being the locomotive engineer, and we are the hired hand shoveling coal into the fire to keep the train going. Oh, and the damsel in distress; that's everyone that we've hurt by cooperating with Satan. The hero, of course, is Jesus Christ, but He doesn't only save the victims of our attacks, He saves *us* from our life of bondage; of throwing the fuel onto Satan's fires.

Satan only gains power over us if we let him. This is because Christ has already defeated Satan at the cross, so his power to control us is limited only to our time on this earth. Every decision that we make is either a godly one or an ungodly one. Think about the last time you participated in something with someone else. Was it honoring to God, or was it not? Did it help someone in need, or did it hurt someone in need? Was it a selfless act, or a selfish act? This is where Satan gets a foothold on us, that can turn into a stronghold if we're not careful.

As Christians, we should be constantly consulting the Holy Spirit concerning the conduct of our lives. Will we make mistakes sometimes and regret our decisions? Satan's still operating the sin train, right? But even Satan has a boss. We have a direct connection to the owner of the train; to God, Himself. Nothing that Satan does can be done without God's knowledge.

David's poor decisions start long before he notices Bathsheba bathing. David sends Joab out with Israel's army rather than go out himself. This is David's first mistake. In ancient Israel, and in most cultures that were governed under a monarchy of that time, the King would be out with his troops on the battlefield. He may not necessarily be leading the fight (more than likely, he and his head generals would be positioned behind all of his troops on a hilltop overlooking the battlefield and combat progress), but nonetheless, he would be there supporting his troops as many of them lose their lives for the kingdom. It reminds me of Jesus being there for His church when believers sometimes lose *their* lives for His kingdom. If David hadn't been hanging around the rooftops of his castle in the middle of the night, when he should have been on the battlefield instead, the sin train would have never left the station.

After that, we know from the narrative that David was told that the late-night bathing beauty was married to one of David's soldiers, yet he sent for her anyway. They committed adultery, she went home and later realized that she was pregnant. The sin train has just left the station.

Author Beth Moore writes in her book, *A Heart Like His*:

> *We may wish we could get everything we want until we look at David and Bathsheba. The gap between wanting and getting is where we must flex the muscle of self-control to protect ourselves. David had risen to a position where his every wish was someone else's command. He had ceased to hear a very important word. The word "no."*[313]

David was probably like many of us. We can easily say no to some things, but not so much to other things. The difference with David is that he knew he had power because of his position; he failed to recognize at that time that he only had power because of God. Nathan the Prophet had to come to *him* to get David to admit his mistake. And, Nathan wasn't concerned as much about David's initial sin of promiscuity, as he was with the fact that David's train was charging full-speed ahead (see 2 Samuel 12:1-15).

David had sinned in multiple ways; at least three different ways regarding his relationship with Bathsheba. First, David sinned in mind—He saw Bathsheba bathing and *thought* she was beautiful. Second, David sinned in word—If we don't confess and repent of the sins in our minds, we will naturally move on to the next phase of sin, the next train station; David opened his mouth and asked who she was and then asked to have her sent to him (see 2 Samuel 11:2-3). Finally, David sinned in deed —having slept with Bathsheba producing a child, whom God would take away from both of them as a form of punishment for their unrighteous behavior. He then went a step further and had Bathsheba's husband killed in battle, thinking that would cover his tracks, but it didn't because God saw everything and revealed it to the Prophet Nathan. That was the final stop, or one might say, "derailment" of the sin train.

There is hope in this tragic story for us though. David was still a man after God's own heart. Unlike unrepentant sinners, or many unbelievers, David shows regret and repentance for his evil actions:

---

[313] Moore, *A Heart Like His*, 180.

*Have mercy on me, O God, according to your unfailing love; according to your great compassion blot out my transgressions. Wash away all my iniquity and cleanse me from my sin. For I know my transgressions, and my sin is always before me. Against you, you only, have I sinned and done what is evil in your sight, so you are right in your verdict and justified when you judge. Surely, I was sinful at birth, sinful from the time my mother conceived me. Yet you desired faithfulness even in the womb; you taught me wisdom in that secret place. Cleanse me with hyssop, and I will be clean; wash me, and I will be whiter than snow. Let me hear joy and gladness; let the bones you have crushed rejoice. Hide your face from my sins and blot out all my iniquity. Create in me a pure heart, O God, and renew a steadfast spirit within me. Do not cast me from your presence or take your Holy Spirit from me. Restore to me the joy of your salvation and grant me a willing spirit, to sustain me.[314]*

The one thing that David did right, was to admit that he had sinned against the Lord. Sometimes, we think that we only need to ask forgiveness from those that we've wronged, but remember, we always wrong God in the process because sin creates further separation from our creator.

I would also like to mention that we see a stark contrast between Uriah and David in this narrative. Uriah's honor put David on the spot. Some theologians would even argue that Uriah had an idea that something was not right when David repeatedly asked him to go home to Bathsheba. Not only was David unmoved by Uriah's integrity, but he also involved others in his army, forcing them to participate in his sin. Remember, David was a man with God's Spirit in him; anointed by Samuel some fifteen years prior. This just goes to show that no matter how close we are to God, none of us are immune to the influences of Satan.

David's sin was lust, and pride, which is a sin we all deal with at one time or another. Perhaps, in a justified irony, God punishes David again at the end of his life using the very thing that David had struggled with all of his life; promiscuity: "The young woman was very beautiful, and she was of service to the king and attended to him, but the king knew her not."[315] That's because he wasn't able *to* "know her," if you get what I mean?

---

[314] Ps. 51:1-12 (ESV).
[315] 1 Kgs. 1:1-4 (ESV).

The moral of the story is, always be on guard spiritually. Satan enjoys drama and seeing us further separate ourselves from the Father. We must trust in Jesus Christ and repent of our sins. Jesus died for our past sins, but until He returns and saves us from the sins of the world, we must ask for forgiveness and actively turn away from sins that take a foothold in our lives. This helps us to be formed into Christlikeness and supports us in our goal of perfection and glorification in Jesus Christ. Remember what the Apostle Peter tells us, *"The enemy, the Devil prowls around like a roaring lion trying to devour us, resist him, standing firm in the faith!"*[316]

It is important to recognize that no one born into this earth is perfect. We all make mistakes. If you've read through this book in its entirety, or if you've read my last book, *Moved by the Spirit*, you surely realize that even I, a pastor, am no exception. But like I've mentioned in other chapters, it's not about being perfected in Christ right now, it's about working towards perfection in Christ; recognizing the union that we've already received through our faith in Jesus Christ.

There's a reason that incense had to burn day and night in the Holy of Holies area inside of the great tabernacle in the wilderness during the time of Moses. It's because even the high priest needed a daily covering for his sins. As God would look down from the cloud into the Holy of Holies, the incense would inhibit His view. The incense represented Christ's blood atonement that covers us, so that we too, are obstructing God's view of our sinful nature. The high priest of the Old Covenant was looked upon by God through the filter of Jesus Christ. For those who have placed their trust and hope in Christ Jesus, God no longer sees them as they see themselves, or as the world sees them; God sees us as a finished product in His beloved son.

*Conclusion*

God dwells, not in a building, but inside each one of us who place our trust in His Son. A few years after I had started pastoring at the small church I serve at now, we had the unfortunate experience of dealing with our district president, who, unbeknownst to me, was in the process of taking our church building away from us. Some have even called him, "A wolf

---

[316] 1 Pet. 5:8-9 (ESV).

in sheep's clothing." Yet, through that experience, I was reminded that it's not about a building; it's about the people inside of the building.

Indeed, what man intends for evil, God turns into good. Sometimes, as I drive past our old church home, I think about my nice office with lots of decorations and bookcases. I miss the pews and the fireside room. I miss the kitchen and the grand piano that I loved to play into the late hours of the night. But, if I had all of those things and no souls to shepherd, I'd just be preaching to an empty building and playing to an absent crowd. Perhaps, that's what God was trying to teach us through that experience. We're not just empty vessels, dead to the world around us, on the contrary, our bodies house the very Spirit of God inside of them; that's where the God of the universe dwells. We *are* the church.

If I could leave you with a final piece of advice, it would be to always remember who you are in Christ; who you represent when you're out in a world constantly trying to bring you down. Don't allow the devil to devour you, for you have been bought at a price. Let not your hearts be troubled, for Christ is always with you, always working at removing the dross from your life; molding you into the mature Christian that He knows you can be. Don't give up when times are hard, because they surely will be. If Satan had given up after the Fall, do you think so many would be led astray? You have the light inside of you to overcome the darkness; let your light shine so brightly that even the world takes notice.

*The End*

# BIBLIOGRAPHY

"An Exegetical Commentary on the Greek New Testament." Pumpkin Cottage Ministry Resources. Accessed March 4, 2020. http://www.lectionarystudies.com/studyn/sunday21baen.html

Andrews, Alan. *The Kingdom Life: A Practical Theology of Discipleship and Spiritual Formation.* Colorado Springs: NavPress, 2010.

Anselm. *Meditation on Fear.* Quoted in Richard H. Schmidt. *God Seekers.* Grand Rapids: Eerdmans, 2008.

Arndt, William, Frederick W. Danker, and Walter Bauer. *A Greek-English Lexicon of the New Testament and Other Early Christian Literature.* Chicago: University of Chicago Press, 2000.

Bakke, Jeannette A. *Holy Invitations: Exploring Spiritual Direction.* Grand Rapids: Baker, 2000.

Ballou, Hosea. *The ancient history of universalism: from the time of the apostles.* Charleston: BiblioLife, 2008.

Barton, Bruce B., David Veerman, and Neil S. Wilson, *1 Timothy, 2 Timothy, Titus: Life Application Bible Commentary.* Wheaton: Tyndale House Publishers, 1993.

Barton, Bruce B., and Grant R. Osborne. *1 & 2 Corinthians: Life Application Bible Commentary.* Wheaton: Tyndale House, 1999.

Barton, Bruce B., and Philip Wesley Comfort. *Ephesians: Life Application Bible Commentary.* Wheaton: Tyndale House Publishers, 1996.

Benner, David G. & Gary W. Moon. *Spiritual Direction and the Care of Souls: A guide to Christian Approaches and Practices.* Downers Grove: InterVarsity Press, 2004.

Boa, Kenneth. *Conformed to His Image: Biblical and Practical Approaches to Spiritual Formation.* Grand Rapids: Zondervan, 2001.

Brown, Brené. *Rising Strong.* New York: Spiegel & Grau, 2015.

Brown, Brené. "The Power of Vulnerability." TEDx Houston. January 3, 2011. https://www.youtube.com/watch?v=iCvmsMzlF7o.

Bubeck, Mark I. *The Adversary: The Christian Versus Demon Activity.* Chicago: Moody Publishers, 2013.

Carlson, Kent & Mike Lueken. *Renovation of the Church: What Happens When a Seeker Church Discovers Spiritual Formation.* Downers Grove: IVP, 2011.

Carson, D.A. *New Dictionary of Biblical Theology.* Downers Grove: IVP, 2000.

Chan, Simon. *Spiritual Theology: A Systematic Study of the Christian Life.* Downers Grove: IVP, 1998.

Cleveland, Christina. *Disunity in Christ: Uncovering the Hidden Forces That Keep Us Apart.* Downers Grove: IVP, 2013.

Coate, Ian. "Christianity: Business or Pleasure?" Relationship Illustrations. Free Christian Illustrations. Accessed October 23, 2017. http://www.freechristianillustrations.com/relationships.html.

Cooper, Dr. Jordan. "Progressive Sanctification: A Lutheran

Doctrine." Just and Sinner.com. April 7, 2013.
http://www.justandsinner.com.

Deere, Jack S. *Surprised by the Voice of God: How God Speaks Today Through Prophecies, Dreams, and Visions.* Grand Rapids: Zondervan, 1998.

Detweiler, Craig. *IGods: How Technology Shapes our Spiritual and Social Lives.* Grand Rapids: Brazos, 2013.

Eastman, Dick. *The Hour That Changes the World.* Nashville: Baker Academic, 1978.

Eckhardt, John. *Fasting: For Breakthrough and Deliverance.* Lake Mary: Charisma House, 2014.

"Ephesians 4." Expositor's Greek Testament. Bible Hub. Accessed February 25, 2020.
https://biblehub.com/commentaries/expositors/ephesians/4.htm.

Feil, Dr. Barbara. "Sorting out a Biblical Response to Gender and Sexuality in our World Today." PowerPoint Presentation. Slide 4. Accessed October 1, 2019.
https://learn.multnomah.edu/courses/5907/files/286800?module_item_id=105806.

Foster, Richard J. *Prayer: Finding the Heart's True Home.* New York: HarperCollins, 1992.

Foster, Richard J. *Streams of Living Water: Celebrating the Great Traditions of Christian Faith.* New York: Harper One, 2001.

Frangipane, Francis. *Unity.* Cedar Rapids: Arrow Publishing, 2015.

Fretheim, Terence E. *God and World in the Old Testament: A Relational Theology of Creation.* Nashville: Abingdon Press, 2005.

Gonzalez, Justo. *The Story of Christianity: The Early Church to the Dawn of the Reformation: Vol. I.* New York: Harper One, 2010.

Grenz, Stanley, J. *Theology for the Community of God.* Grand Rapids: Eerdmans, 1994.

Grudem, Wayne. *Systematic Theology: An Introduction to Biblical Doctrine.* Grand Rapids: Zondervan, 1994.

Hayford, Jack. *Living the Spirit-Formed Life: Growing in the 10 Principles of Spirit-Filled Discipleship.* Minneapolis: Chosen, 2017.

Henry, Matthew. *Matthew Henry's Commentary on the Whole Bible: Complete and Unabridged in One Volume.* Peabody: Hendrickson, 1994.

Holmes, Urban T. III. *A History of Christian Spirituality: An Analytical Introduction.* Harrisburg: Morehouse, 2002.

Houston, James. "The History of Spiritual Discipline." Open Biola. April 25, 2017. https://www.youtube.com/watch?v=aY2s6KDnGII&feature=youtu.be.

Hughes, Robert B. & J. Carl Laney. *Tyndale Concise Bible Commentary. The Tyndale Reference Library.* Wheaton: Tyndale House Publishers, 2001.

Ingraham, Chip. *The Invisible War: What Every Believer Needs to Know about Satan, Demons, & Spiritual Warfare.* Nashville: Baker Books, 2015.

Isaacson, Walter. *Steve Jobs.* New York: Simon and Schuster, 2011.

James, Bryan Smith & Lynda Graybeal. *A Spiritual Formation*

*Workbook: Small Group Resources for Nurturing Christian Growth.*
New York: Harper One, 1999.

Jamieson, Robert, A. R. Fausset, and David Brown. *Commentary Critical and Explanatory on the Whole Bible.* Vol. 2. Oak Harbor, WA: Logos Research Systems, Inc., 1997.

Jobes, Karen H. *Letters to the Church: A Survey of Hebrews and the General Epistles.* Grand Rapids: Zondervan, 2011.

Johnson, Alan F. *1 Corinthians, Vol. 7, The IVP New Testament Commentary Series.* Westmont: IVP Academic, 2004.

Johnson, Darrell W. *Fifty-Seven Words That Change the World: A Journey Through the Lord's Prayer.* Vancouver: Regent College Publishing, 2005.

Johnson, Sharon. "Therapist Guide to Clinical Intervention." PowerPoint Presentation. The website for NIMH – National Institute for Mental Health, 2004. https://www.nimh.nih.gov/index.shtml.

Keaton, Mark. *The Lexham Propositional Outlines Glossary.* Bellingham, WA: Lexham Press, 2014.

Kline, Donald L. *Susanna Wesley: God's Catalyst for Revival.* Lima: C.S.S. Publishing, 1980.

Liefeld, Walter L. Ephesians. Vol. 10. *The IVP New Testament Commentary Series.* Downers Grove: InterVarsity Press, 1997.

Lukaszewski, Albert L. & Mark Dubis. *The Lexham Syntactic Greek New Testament: Expansions and Annotations.* Logos Bible Software, 2009. Eph. 4.

Lynch, John, Bruce McNicol, and Bill Thrall. *The Cure: What if God isn't who you think He is and neither are you?* Phoenix: Trueface, 2011.

Moore, Beth. *A Heart Like His: Intimate Reflections on the Life of David.* Nashville: B&H, 2012.

Morgan, Christopher & Robert Peterson. *Fallen: A Theology of Sin.* Wheaton: Crossway, 2013.

Parsons, John. J. "Hebrew Names of God," Hebrew4Christians.com. Accessed October 20, 2017. http://www.hebrew4christians.com/Names_of_G-d/Spirit_of_God/spirit_of_god.html.

Piper, John. *Reading the Bible Supernaturally: Seeing and Savoring the Glory of God in Scripture.* Wheaton: Crossway, 2017.

"Prayer Power." Word Press. Accessed October 23, 2017. http://prayer-power.com/prayer-relationships/.

Richter, Sandra. *The Epic of Eden: A Christian Entry into the Old Testament.* Downers Grove: IVP, 2008.

Runge, Steven E. *The Lexham Discourse Greek New Testament: Glossary.* Lexham Press, 2008.

Schmidt, Richard H. *God Seekers.* Grand Rapids: Eerdmans, 2008.

Simpson, Amy. *Troubled Minds.* Downers Grove: IVP, 2013.

Thrall, Bill. *Communities of Grace.* Quoted in Alan Andrews, *The Kingdom Life: A Practical Theology of Discipleship and Spiritual Formation.* Colorado Springs: NavPress, 2010.

Thompson, Curt. *Anatomy of the Soul.* Carol Stream: Tyndale Momentum, 2010.

Vincent, Marvin R. *Word Studies in the New Testament.* Vol. 1. New York: Charles Scribner's Sons, 1887.

Wallace, Daniel. *Greek Grammar: Beyond the Basics.* Grand Rapids: Zondervan, 1996.

"What does 'When the Perfect Comes' Mean in 1 Corinthians 13:9-10?" Bible.org. January 1, 2001. https://bible.org/question/what-does-"when-perfect-comes"-mean-1-corinthians-139-10.

"What is Lent and Why Does it Last Forty Days?" Ask the UMC. Accessed April 21, 2020. https://www.umc.org/en/content/ask-the-umc-what-is-lent-and-why-does-it-last-forty-days.

"What is OneCry?" OneCry: A Nationwide Call for Spiritual Awakening. Accessed May 13, 2020. https://onecry.com/about/.

Whitefield, Samuel. "The Adamic Covenant." Samuel Whitefield.com. March 22, 2013. https://samuelwhitefield.com/591/the-adamic-covenant.

Whitney, Donald S. *Simplify Your Spiritual Life: Spiritual Disciplines for the Overwhelmed.* Colorado Springs: NavPress, 2003.

Willard, Dallas. "Spiritual Formation: What it is, and How it is done." Accessed January 7, 2020. http://www.dwillard.org/articles/individual/spiritual-formation-what-it-is-and-how-it-is-done.

Willard, Dallas. *The Spirit of the Disciplines: Understanding How God Changes Lives.* New York: HarperCollins, 1991.

# Afterword

Writing this book has truly been an amazing journey for me. Thank you for taking the time to read it. My hope is that you have gained something practical and useful from your reading. Spiritual formation is a process, and I hope that my stories and experiences in the area of spiritual formation have given you a basic guide map—or at least a starting point to begin your journey in faith with the beloved Jesus Christ. My goal is always to glorify God with my writing, and I hope that I've honored Him properly with this volume.

As mentioned, a few times within the text already, at the time of writing this book, the nation was faced with the disastrous Covid-19 pandemic. Many people lost their jobs, many employers lost their businesses, and many others lost their lives to the horrific Coronavirus. It's important to let people know that they are not alone in their fight against the invisible enemy. God is always there with you, every step of the way. You win some battles; you lose some battles, but Jesus has already won with war. Michael, one of my old college classmates said it best, "There are certain things that are invisible that can kill you, but there's also something invisible that can save you." Jesus saves us from our eternal death, and that's more powerful than any enemy that comes against us.

The second impact on our society is that of racial disparity and injustice. While racial tension has plagued the US since the time our country's inception, only recently have people of color taken an active stand against injustices that they face. The deaths of our African American brothers has sparked a revolution in the way that we address police brutality and racism in our country. Being a middle-class, white person who has never experienced my skin color working against me, I cannot speak on behalf of the African American community; however, we all must honor Jesus' words to love one another. With clear divisiveness amongst even our Christian brothers and sisters, I would encourage all of us to speak less and listen more. And always remember, social media may make it seem like the world is falling apart, but if you set your phone down and look outside, the sun is still shining.

Long ago, Cain murdered his brother Abel out of bitterness and jealousy towards him. Indeed, God didn't accept Cain's offering because Cain's heart was hardened. Reflecting upon the Cain and Abel story in Genesis, Jesus says this in addressing hatred towards our brothers and sisters: "Therefore, if you are offering your gift at the altar and there remember that your brother or sister has something against you, leave your gift there in front of the altar. First, go and be reconciled to them; then come and offer your gift."[317] Perhaps, we must remember to reconcile ourselves with our brothers and sisters *before* we approach the Holy God.

I've personally struggled with many things throughout my life. From pride and self-esteem issues, to sexual addiction and depression. Yet, I've never hesitated to look up to the heavens and ask for God's help. We must be humble enough to admit that we need someone stronger than ourselves to help rescue us from Satan's influence. The Lord has delivered me from so many of Satan's footholds; so many of my own reckless decisions, that I could never, ever repay Him. But that's how God is. He's not looking for us to repay Him, for, how could we? He's looking for us to love Him, to accept Jesus Christ into our hearts, and to obey His commands.

Recently, I've been spending a lot more time in contemplative prayer with the Father—asking Him for advice on certain career choices, thanking Him for keeping my wife and children safe and healthy through the pandemic that to date, has killed more than six hundred thousand people worldwide. Some members of the community have inquired of my thoughts about being quarantined, and wearing a mask in public, and so forth. My response to them has been that we should be strong in our faith that God will protect us, but we also must be wise about our choices. Do I risk interrupting God's will for a long and prosperous life of a fellow image-bearer because I wasn't wearing a mask and didn't realize that I was asymptomatic?

---

[317] Matt. 5:23-24 (NIV).

Or do I use wisdom in listening to God to discern what He has placed upon my heart?

In my thirty-something year relationship with Jesus Christ, I've come to discover that it's a balance between my actions and God's sovereignty. Sometimes, regardless of my actions, God's will is going to prevail. Many times, as a result of my actions in obedience to Him, things turn out better for me than I could have ever imagined. And still, other times, when I've gone against God's desires for my life regarding decision making, it has always ended up consequential for me. Every. Single. Time. The heart of a man plans his way but the Lord directs his steps.

I pray that you have been able to recognize some of the areas in your spiritual walk with Christ that are going well, and others that you may need to nurture to build up your trust and strengthen your relationship with Him. Jesus is always in your corner, advocating for you, cheering you on, interceding for you, and loving you. He knows everything about you, so be sure and learn everything you can about Him. You only have your lifetime, however short or long that may be, to accept Him into your heart—if you haven't done so already.

I've included in the appendix a few of the assignments that I completed for my Seminary courses in Spiritual Formation and Spiritual Warfare. One is a small group study that is designed for ten weeks and focuses primarily on spiritual formation exercises and questions that any small group leader can ask of the group. The other, perhaps even more essential, is a ten-week preaching series on spiritual warfare. I encourage you to utilize these exercises as they will surely help you in your otherworldly battles.

Blessings to you, dear brothers and sisters in Christ. I'm so honored and humbled that you have chosen to spend your time with me learning about modern spiritual formation. My prayer is that you continue to walk towards Christ, leaving all fear and doubt behind, and utilizing the Holy Spirit to move closer to the person that God has designed you to be. Only then, can you truly be *Transformed by the Spirit.*

*Craig Prather*

# Appendix 1

Spiritual Formation Bible Study Series:

*Ten Week Small Group Study for Nurturing Spiritual Growth*

*Week One:*

**Topic:** Introduction to Spiritual Formation/The Life of Jesus Christ

**Purpose Statement:** To discover a balanced vision of Christian faith and practice

**Opening:** We will begin spending a few minutes (up to five) in silent prayer.

**Relevant Scriptures:** Col. 3:13, Eph. 4:31-32, John 8:28, Ps. 86:11, 2 Cor. 13:5, John 15:15, John 15:14

Jesus Christ functions in four main ways in the Christian's life: Savior, Teacher, Lord, and Friend. In our relationship with him, each of us experiences some of these roles more powerfully than others. Which role have you experienced the most and do you understand the best? In which would you like to see yourself grow stronger?

The previous question reveals two things about us. 1) We are often quite familiar with <u>one</u> way that God works in our lives. 2) We are often unfamiliar with <u>other ways</u> God works in our lives. We should be thankful that God works in our lives in such profound ways.

**Exercise 1**: Identifying Our Strengths and Weaknesses

Based on the six traditions of the Church/Spiritual life, identify the areas that you consider your greatest strength. Which do you consider your weakest? Use a scale of 1-10 next to each category (1-being least proficient).

1. Holiness (having pure thoughts, words, and actions/overcoming temptation)

2. Contemplative (spending time with God in prayer and meditation)

3. Incarnational (unifying the sacred-secular areas of my life)

4. Charismatic (welcoming the Holy Spirit while nurturing my spiritual gifts)

5. Social Justice (helping others less fortunate than I)

6. Evangelical (sharing the gospel of Jesus Christ, and reading scriptures)[318]

*Week Two*

**Topic:** Disciplined Prayer

**Purpose Statement:** To use this hour of prayer time to focus on twelve separate, yet vital areas of prayer, and to further deepen our relationship with Christ.

**Opening:** We will begin spending a few moments (up to five) in silent prayer.

**Relevant Scriptures:** John 17, Luke 6:12

The twelve-step prayer plan in this book should be applied with spiritual liberty rather than regimented legality. After using these steps for several days or weeks, allow your own prayer program to develop.

---

[318] James & Graybeal, *A Spiritual Formation Workbook*, 25-31.

# The Hour That Changes the World

In his book, *The Hour That Changes the World*, Dick Eastman suggests that one divide an hour into 12 periods of 5 minutes each, during which you focus on one form of prayer. After 5 minutes, move on to the next form of prayer.

## Group Questions:

- What was the hardest category to pray for and why?

- What was the easiest category to pray for and why?

- Did Satan attempt to distract you while engaged in these prayers, if yes, how so?

- Did the time seem to go by fast or slow? Were you surprised by that?[319]

---

[319] Eastman, *The Hour That Changes the World*, 58.

**Topic:** The Virtuous Life

**Purpose Statement:** To realize that holiness is important to God; therefore, it should be important to us.

**Opening:** We will begin spending a few moments (up to five) in silent prayer.

**Relevant Scriptures:** Matthew 4:1-11, Exod. 20:2-17, Matt. 19:17

**Exercise 1:** Pray for the Holy Spirit to purify your heart and mind, then listen

In bringing about change, God works from the inside out and he works through the Holy Spirit. Like last week's prayer exercise, set aside a one-hour time block for deep and heartfelt prayer. During that time, ask God to purify your heart and mind through the power of the Holy Spirit.

**Exercise 2:** Respond to temptation with the Word of God

Jesus overcame the devil's temptations by holding fast to God's commandments. Respond to the temptation with the following verses: Deut. 8:3; 6:16; 6:13. Jesus used the power of God through the Scripture to defeat the devil, and so can we

**Exercise 3:** Taming of the tongue

In the morning, ask the Holy Spirit to "set a guard over your mouth" (Ps. 141:3), preventing you from saying anything negative. Be ruthless about this! Do not let even the slightest hint of criticism or judgment come out of your mouth. Search for ways to be positive about everything around you and be ready to give compliments as often as you can.

**Exercise 4:** A day without saying anything dishonest

Jesus said of Nathaniel that he was a person without "guile" (John 1:47, KJV). What a compliment! Guile is dishonesty, deceit, double-talk, falsehood, shading the truth, manipulating words, etc. Pray that the Spirit will make your heart pure and honest and alert you to anything less than forthright. Do not manipulate your words; let your "yes" be "yes" and your "no" be "no."

**Group Questions:**

1. What was the easiest exercise to complete and why?

2. What was the most difficult exercise to complete and why?

3. Were you able to go an entire day without saying anything negative?

4. Were you able to go an entire day without saying anything dishonest?[320]


*Week Four*

**Topic:** Fasting

**Purpose Statement:** To be aware that fasting not only gives glory to God by resisting earthly desires, but it replaces that time with prayer, strengthening your spirit.

**Opening:** We will begin spending a few moments (up to five) in silent prayer.

**Relevant Scriptures:** Esther 4:16, Luke 18:11-12, Isa. 58, Ps. 35:13

**Exercise 1:** Approach fasting with humility and sincerity

In Jesus's day, the Pharisees fasted with attitudes of pride and superiority. Anytime you are full of pride, being legalistic and religious, you can fast and pray all you want, but you won't see many miracles. We must approach fasting with humility. Fasting must be genuine and not religious or hypocritical. Before beginning your partial fast, pray that the Holy Spirit gives you a

---

[320] James & Graybeal, *A Spiritual Formation Workbook*, 37-42.

heart of humility and the strength to honor God during your fasting.

**Exercise 2:** Declare the benefits of fasting over your life

Prior to fasting, declare the following prayers:

- Lord, I believe in the power of your chosen fast

- Lord, let my fasting destroy the yokes that the enemy has set up against me

- Let your light come into my life through your chosen fast

- Let health and healing be released to me through your chosen fast

- Let me see breakthroughs of salvation and deliverance in my life through your chosen fast

- Let miracles be released in my life through your chosen fast

- Let your power and authority be released in my life through your chosen fast

**Exercise 3**: Try a 24-hour partial fast

Jesus fasted in the wilderness to gain spiritual strength. When we fast, we are saying no to the uncontrolled appetites of our body and thereby gaining mastery over them. The practice of fasting also reveals hidden traits such as anger, selfishness, laziness, etc. After eating lunch on the first day, do not eat a full meal until lunch on the second day. During the 24 hours, drink plenty of water.

**Group Questions:**

1. Was it easier to start with a partial day fast or an entire 24-hour fast and why?

2. Did your fasting time reveal to you your spiritual strengths and weaknesses?

3. How did feel the fasting benefited you?

*4.* Could you continue to fast regularly? Why or why not?[321]


*Week Five*

**Topic:** The Spirit-Empowered Life

**Purpose Statement:** To realize that as believers, we are temples in whom the Holy Spirit dwells. We are empowered by the Spirit to share the gospel that convicts and converts, to bear the fruit of the gospel in our lives, and to exercise special gifts that enable us to build up the Church.

**Opening:** We will begin spending a few moments (up to five) in silent prayer.

**Relevant Scriptures:** John 14:15-17, 1 Cor. 3:16; 6:19; 2 Cor. 6:16, Gal. 5:22, 1 Cor. 12:1-11

Without the Holy Spirit, it would be impossible to practice the Six Traditions. The Spirit spurs the believer to pray and meditate (the focus of the Contemplative Tradition); to seek the virtuous life (the Holiness Tradition); to exercise mercy and compassion to one another (the Social Justice Tradition); to proclaim the gospel as found in the Scriptures (the Evangelical Tradition), and to promote harmony between our faith and our work (the Incarnational Tradition). God wants us to be active in our lives; to endow us with supernatural abilities; to see us live with love, joy, peace, etc. (the Charismatic Tradition).

**Exercise 1:** Yield to the work of the Spirit

Spend one hour in prayer this week specifically asking the Spirit to begin working in your life in a new and powerful way. Remember, you are seeking God. Make no demands; have no expectations. Your only task is to surrender yourself to God. This may lead to a time of confession.

---

[321] Eckhardt, *Fasting*, 4-25.

**Exercise 2**: Nurture the fruit of the Spirit

Galatians 5:22 lists nine virtues called the fruit of the Spirit. Set aside fifteen minutes a day to meditate on the fruit of the Spirit. Ask God to show you which virtue needs to be more evident in your life. Then ask the Holy Spirit to begin working in your mind and heart, knowing that change will come through sustained communion with God.

**Group Questions:**

1. Which of the following best describes the work of the Spirit in your life? Explain your selection.

   a. The Spirit has not been a major part of my spiritual life.

   b. I am beginning to see signs of the Spirit's presence in my life.

2. What do you do to set the stage for the Holy Spirit to work in your heart?

3. Do you pray to the Holy Spirit before and after you read the Scriptures?[322]

4. Have you asked the Spirit to reveal what's in your heart?

*Week Six*

**Topic:** The Compassionate Life

**Purpose Statement:** To be aware that one of the most remarkable aspects of practicing the Social Justice Tradition is its double effect of helping others, and in turn, we help ourselves.

**Opening:** We will begin spending a few moments (up to five) in silent prayer.

---

[322] James & Graybeal, *A Spiritual Formation Workbook*, 44-50.

**Relevant Scriptures:** Matt. 25:31-46, 1 John 4:11, Prov. 14:31, Micah 6:8

**Exercise 1:** Write a kind, encouraging letter

This may seem like a small task, but it can work miracles. Take time to write a letter that tells someone how important he or she is to you. We seldom let people know how much they are appreciated. Or perhaps you know someone who is struggling with something, a decision, a failed marriage, a disappointment. Write a letter that tells him or her that you care and that you are available to talk or listen.

**Exercise 2:** Volunteer to help at a local food bank or soup kitchen

Relief efforts and service organizations always need helping hands. Look in the telephone book or ask someone in the church for the name of a food bank or soup kitchen. Call and volunteer to help in any area. Such organizations usually need workers to stock shelves, serve food, clean storerooms, do clerical work, and undertake other such tasks.

**Exercise 3:** Guard the reputation of another person

Although you cannot see it, a person's reputation is valuable, and you can guard and protect it by refusing to gossip or backbite. By refusing to take part in discussions that focus on half-truths or fault-finding, you can contribute to the death of a rumor or criticism. Your gentle demeanor and response in protecting another person's valuable reputation can help others become aware of the harmful nature of their words.

**Exercise 4:** Take a stand

Is there racism, sexism, or some other form of discrimination in a club or business or a community or institution that you need to address? If so, discuss with the Spiritual Formation Group what your response should be.

**Group Questions:**

1. What did you learn about God and yourself while doing this exercise?

2. Have you ever been a stranger? Describe some of the feelings you had.

3. Have you ever been unjustly treated? How did you respond?[323]


*Week Seven*

**Topic:** A Word-Centered Life

**Purpose Statement:** To realize that God uses three central ways to reveal himself to us: the written word, the living Word, and the spoken word.

**Opening:** We will begin spending a few moments (up to five) in silent prayer.

**Relevant Scriptures:** Luke 4:16-20; 42-44, John 1:1, Rom. 10:17

**Exercise 1:** Memorize a verse of Scripture

Select a verse unfamiliar to you from a favorite translation. You may want to pick: Gal. 2:20, Rom. 5:1, John 3:16, Psalm 1:1, Eph. 2:8, or some other verse. Memorizing Scripture allows God's word to take root in your thought-life and your inner heart.

**Exercise 2:** Meditate on a verse or brief passage about Jesus Christ

Keep your selection simple. Take twenty minutes or so to read the verse or passage slowly and carefully. Pause after each sentence and reflect on it. Ask questions: What does this sentence mean? What is God telling me about Himself? What is God telling me about myself?

**Exercise 3:** Look for an opportunity to tell someone about your faith

Prayer precedes these opportunities, so begin by praying that God will bring you into contact with someone who needs to hear about Jesus. Ask God to let you know in some way who is the right person and when is the right time. Do not speak in a way that makes that person feel like he or she is being judged. Simply express what has happened to you and let that word

---

[323] Ibid., 51-58.

go forth simply and honestly.

**Exercise 4:** Proclaim the gospel by your actions

St. Francis reminds us, "Always preach Christ; use words when necessary." During the next few days let your actions speak for you, but before beginning, pray for the insight to see your life as others see it. Then as you come into contact with people, pay particular attention to your actions and what they are conveying. By the end of this exercise, you should be able to pick out areas in your life that speak well of Christ and areas that need correcting.

**Group Questions:**

- What did you learn about God and about yourself while doing the exercise?

- How has the proclamation of the gospel of Jesus Christ influenced your life?

- Does the concept that the Evangelical Traditional includes the written word, the living Word, and the proclamation of the gospel help or hinder you?[324]

*Week Eight*

**Topic:** The Sacramental Life

**Purpose Statement:** To realize that the Trinity is at the heart of the Incarnational Tradition because Christ is the Incarnation. In the person of Jesus Christ, God became human, thereby putting his blessings upon the material, physical world in which we live.

**Opening:** We will begin spending a few moments (up to five) in silent prayer.

---

[324] Ibid., 59-66.

**Relevant Scriptures:** Luke 13:10-17, Luke 2:22-24, Rom. 7:15

As physical beings we find it easy to focus on the material, the things we can see and touch. This presents a huge problem when we start exploring the world of the spirit. We cannot smell, taste, touch, see or hear the spiritual, so we hesitate to believe it's real. The Holy Spirit helps us to overcome this disunity by promoting the harmony of the physical and the spiritual.

**Exercise 1:** Take an inventory of your life

List on a piece of paper all of the activities that you are involved in, such as work, church, clubs, housework, parenting, hobbies, sports, etc. Decide how well you bring the presence of God into each activity. Do not be discouraged if the results are disappointing. Even for people who have been practicing the disciplines for quite a while, change takes time.

**Exercise 2:** Remove the barrier that keeps God outside

As you sit in a chair, imagine that you have an extra layer of skin that keeps God's Spirit out of the innermost parts of your being. Hold this image in your mind for a moment. Then destroy or rip off the barrier and invite the Spirit of God to penetrate you, to overwhelm you with his love, to take up permanent residence in your body, to make a "tabernacle." Continue sitting quietly until you feel that the work is complete, expressing your gratitude when it is done.

**Group Questions:**

- Do you ever feel guilty for doing work on what many consider a "holy" day, such as Sunday or Easter or Christmas?

- How do you think you would respond if your pastor stopped speaking to heal a woman? Or if a homeless person walked down the aisle during the middle of a choir number and asked the pastor for money to rent an apartment?

- Have you ever considered that the everyday aspects of your life are as important to God as the spiritual aspects?

- How does it make you feel to think that God works through you to do his work in the world? [325]


*Week Nine*

**Topic:** Spiritual Warfare

**Purpose Statement:** To make Christians aware that their daily lives are influenced by the subtle deception and lies of our adversary.

**Opening:** We will begin spending a few moments (up to five) in silent prayer.

**Relevant Scriptures:** Eph. 6:10-12, 2 Kings 6:15-19, Dan. 10, 2 Cor. 10:3-5

Our responsibility is to become acutely aware of Satan's methods but not be preoccupied with them. We do not fight for victory; we fight from victory. As believers in Christ, we are invincible. The Bible has given us numerous promises of victory over the power of the enemy. We may not know much about spiritual battles when we first realize they exist, but we can at least know that it's not about our ability to muster up our own strength. The only way to win this war is to be strong in the Lord.

**Five Specific Times You Can Expect Spiritual Attack:**

- Spiritual Growth – Satan attacks us when we're taking significant steps of faith for spiritual growth.

- Invading Enemy Territory – A second time we may be attacked is when we're invading enemy territory. Getting involved in evangelism by sharing your faith, going on a mission trip, etc.

- Exposing the Enemy – The third instance when Satan attacks directly is when we're exposing him for who he really is.

---

[325] Ibid., 67-73.

- Breaking with the World – A fourth example of a high probability for an attack is when we repent and make a clean break with the world, a long-held pattern of sin, or an unholy relationship.

- Blessings to Come – The fifth occasion for an attack is when God is preparing us individually or corporately for a great work for his glory.

Don't let these things scare you. That's exactly what the adversary wants. The blessings of being used by God to impact the world always far outweigh the harassments of the enemy. You have to choose between fear and faith.

**Exercise 1:** Evaluate your heart

What's in your heart? In what area of your life has God spoken his truth to you that you are not currently following? Have you opened your heart to demonic activity in any way? Evaluate the areas God has shown you that you have let become idols in your life. Perhaps you watch too much television, or eat too much food, or have unresolved marital issues? Whatever God has shown you, regardless of your fear, take the first step. Once you do, he'll give you grace. If he has shown you to do something, he will give you power and grace to do it. The breastplate of righteousness is not that difficult to put on when God is helping us.

**Group Questions:**

1. Have you ever heard the spiritual armor described as a checklist? How would your spiritual life change if you knew that your protection was a lifestyle instead of a formula?

2. Can you think of times when the enemy has exploited you at your most vulnerable moments?

3. Is there any God-given spiritual territory you have already given up to the enemy? How can you take it back?

4. What activities and responsibilities do you fulfill out of a sense of guilt? What steps can you take to remove the sense of guilt and replace it with a devotion to God?

**5.** Is there anything God has shown you to do that you are not currently doing?

*6.* What statement does our disobedience make about our relationship with God?[326]

*Week Ten*

**Topic:** A Practical Strategy for Spiritual Growth

**Purpose Statement:** To be aware that it is very easy to focus on our needs, our failures, our efforts to "get right" with God, but our worship must center on Christ. Jesus reminds us that our power and authority come from him. When we come together and agree on something, Christ assures us that God will do it.

**Opening:** We will begin spending a few moments (up to five) in silent prayer.

**Relevant Scriptures:** Matt. 18:19-20

Jesus tells his followers that he will be in their midst each time they gather in his name. Far from leaving them on their own, Jesus promises his disciples that he will be with them forever. Christ is with us as well, when we gather "in his name." Because Jesus Christ called us to become disciples, he is always at the center of our corporate gatherings. He is the reason we come together.

**What is a Spiritual Formation Group?**

A few years ago, a Princeton University poll revealed that the number-one priority for most Christians was "personal spiritual growth." Despite this need, most churches do not have intentional plans to meet their members' desires for spiritual growth. Recognizing our own need, we have been tak-

---

[326] Ingraham, *The Invisible War*, 15-65.

ing small steps toward consistent spiritual growth in the previous eight sessions. The Spiritual Formation Group is a Christian fellowship whose purpose is to encourage its members to practice the spiritual disciplines. It is a group that focuses on what God has done, is doing, and will do in our lives as we begin practicing the spiritual disciplines.

**Group Questions:**

- What did you learn about God and about yourself while doing this exercise?

- Why is it so easy to focus on ourselves rather than on what Christ is doing among us?

- Of the three needs listed below, which is your most urgent?

- To grow closer to others

- To be encouraged by others

- To learn from others

- Which of these three pieces do you need the most?

1. Balance and community

2. Structure, ideas, and exercises

3. Encouragement and accountability[327]

---

[327] James & Graybeal, *A Spiritual Formation Workbook*, 74-83.

# Appendix 2

Ten Week Spiritual Warfare Preaching Series.

*Week One*

"Spiritual Strength"

*Ephesians 6:10-11*

**Subject:** How do we overcome the demons that haunt us?

**Compliment:** Through the power of God's strength

**BI:** In contrast to human strength, God is the source and supplier of all spiritual strength through which believers can do all that God asks.

### Introduction:

- We are commanded to be strong in the Lord and to put on the full armor of God because there's a struggle that is not against flesh and blood but is waged on an entirely different level.

### God is the source of spiritual strength

- The word "finally" signals the beginning of Paul's conclusion to his letter, where he will give words of vital importance for his readers. In this letter, Paul explained the need for unity in the body of believers; here he further explained the need for that unity—there will be inevitable clashes with evil, and the church must be ready to stand and fight.

- "Be strong in the Lord" refers to strength derived from God, not strength we humans have to somehow obtain. The words "be strong" describe the continual empowering of the Christian community. God's strength and *his mighty power* are part of the kingdom blessings available to God's people.[328]

**Cross Reference:**

**1. Psalm 68:35**

**Illustration:**

- When I was around sixteen years old, I found myself at a party that involved a lot of alcohol consumption. Unfortunately, there was a college-age guy at the party who, I later found out, was known for getting teenagers to drink and then sexually assaulting them. I was almost his next victim, but thankfully, I prayed that the Lord would give me His strength to sober up and remove myself from the situation. God came through for me immediately after my prayer and I was able to sneak downstairs and remove myself from the house and dangerous situation unnoticed.

**Conclusion:**

- God's strength is much greater than ours. We must put on the whole armor of God in order to stand against the schemes of the devil. Next week, we'll look at who or "what" it is that we are fighting against as we continue our series on Spiritual Warfare.

- Let's pray

---

[328] Barton and Comfort, *Ephesians*, 127–128.

Week Two

"Wrestling Against Evil"

*Ephesians 6:12*

**Subject:** What does the believer wrestle against?

**Compliment:** The rulers and authorities of evil in the world and heavenly places

**BI:** We are wrestling against evil forces that we cannot always see

### Introduction:

We battle against rulers, powers, and world forces of darkness, yet we must stand firm. The world system includes Satan's warfare against God's plans for the believer. The Lord Jesus Christ called Satan, "the prince of this world" (John 12:31). Therefore, we must be aware that Satan will often use the world and earthly desires against us to advance his evil agenda.[329]

### Spiritual Battles

1. The Christians face a *struggle* against evil—describing hand-to-hand combat. But we are not in an earthly military campaign—our battle *is not against enemies of blood and flesh*. Instead, we battle the demons over whom Satan has control. Demons work to tempt people to sin.

2. They were not created by Satan because God is the Creator of all. Rather, the demons are fallen angels who joined Satan in his rebellion and thus became perverted and evil. The descriptive words "rulers," "authorities," "cosmic powers," and

---

[329] Bubeck, *The Adversary*, 54.

"spiritual forces of evil in the heavenly places" reveal the characteristics of these enemies as well as their sphere of operations.

3.       "Rulers and authorities" are cosmic powers, or demons, mentioned in 1:21. These spiritual beings have limited power.[330]

**Illustration:**

• Have you ever walked down Fourth Street late at night, here in Reno? Have you ever driven by it, even? It's almost as if you can feel an evil presence around you. That's because evil does not like to be exposed. Fourth Street is not only the darkest street in Reno, but it's also the most heavily prostituted, and drug active street in our community. I've certainly had my fun out on Fourth Street at local bars and pubs, but now I don't go down there at all, unless there's a detour on one of the other roads, because I know that spiritual forces are active in that area, so why play near the fire?

**Conclusion:**

• Paul knew that the Ephesians were dealing with witchcraft, sorcery, false prophets, gossip, and a host of other sinful behaviors. These are channels or pathways for evil to enter into our lives. We must be aware that what we can't see can hurt us. Next week, we'll look at some of the spiritual weapons to use against our adversary.

• Let's Pray

---

[330] Barton and Comfort, *Ephesians*, 129.

"The Belt of Truth"

*Ephesians 6:13-14b*

**Subject:** How do we stand firm against evil

**Compliment:** By taking up the whole armor of God

**BI:** When doing spiritual battle, start by fastening your belt of truth

### Introduction:

- The real secret to happiness isn't anywhere in prime-time entertainment, of course. The key to a fulfilled life has nothing to do with fast cars, revolving partners, or this year's fashions. Those are just things in which the enemy and the flesh conspire to tempt us. The remedy and number one defense against the devious deception is to clothe ourselves in truth.[331]

### Defensive Pieces of God's Armor

- In order to *stand therefore* in the heat of battle, believers need every piece of God's armor. The order of the pieces listed in the following verses is the order in which a soldier would put them on. First, Paul wrote, *fasten the belt of truth around your waist.* This belt, also called a girdle, was about six inches wide. Probably made of leather, it held together with the clothing underneath as well as holding the other pieces of armor in place, such as the breastplate and the sheath for the sword. It may have contained a "breechclout," an apron that protected the lower abdomen. It may have also braced the back in order to give strength.

- When the belt was fastened, the soldier was "on duty,"

---

[331] Ingram, *The Invisible War*, 92.

ready to fight. A slackened belt meant "off duty." Christians, however, must face each day with a fastened belt, ready to fight the battle when needed.

- As the belt formed the foundation of the soldier's armor, the truth is the foundation of the Christian life. This "truth" refers to the believer's character as a person who can be relied on for the truth. It certainly also refers to the truth of God's Word and his message in the gospel. If we could not be absolutely sure of our faith, if we were not sure that Jesus is "the truth" (John 14:6), then there would be little use for the armor or in attempting to fight any battle. God's truth, as revealed to us through Jesus Christ, forms the foundation of victorious Christian living.

- When the enemy, the father of lies (John 8:44), attacks with his lies, half-truths, and distortions, we believers can stand on the truth we believe. Jesus prayed for his followers: "Sanctify them by Your truth. Your word is truth" (John 17:17 NKJV).[332]

**Illustration:**

- Satan is the author of lies. He has no problem with us lying to God and each other because that will create division amongst us, which is what he wants. Remember what he said to Eve in the garden? That she will surely not die? Guess what, he lied. Anytime I've told a lie, it's come back to haunt me, in either earthly ways, heavenly ways, or both.

**Conclusion:**

- As believers, we are called to a higher standard than the world. This is why Paul says to live a life worthily of our calling (Eph. 4:1, Emphasis mine). If we live a life of lies, what makes

---

[332] Barton and Comfort, *Ephesians*, 131–132.

us different from those who are of the world? We are to be in this world, but not of this world.

- Let's Pray

"The Breastplate of Righteousness"

*Ephesians 6:14c*

**Subject:** How do we achieve right standing before the Father?

**Compliment:** Through faith alone in Christ Jesus

**BI:** Nothing we can do will satisfy God's wrath upon us. Only our faith in Christ will display His righteousness within us.

### Introduction:

- Last week, we looked at the Belt of Truth as the first piece of spiritual equipment to put on. In order, the next piece would be that of the Breastplate of Righteousness that would cover the midsection below the neck to the thighs to protect the heart. We might be tempted to give up if we think that this means we have to become perfect in truth before we can be protected but don't give up just yet.

- The word, "righteousness" means uprightness, right living, integrity in one's lifestyle and character. It is a matter of conforming to God's will through sanctification. It's rooted in objective righteousness that we already possess in our standing before God through Christ's work on the cross.

- The belt of truth has to come first because it is fundamental in our quest to become righteous the way that God already sees us to be, in Christ.[333]

### Defensive Spiritual Armor

- In Isaiah 59:17, God "put on righteousness as his breastplate." Protecting the vital organs, the breastplate was a vital piece in the soldier's armor. No soldier would go into battle without his breastplate. Often this had a back piece too, protecting the body from hits from behind.

- "Righteousness" provides a significant defense; it gives the evidence that we have been made right with God and that this righteousness has been given us by the Holy Spirit. Believers have been made righteous through the blood of Christ. The believers then want to live in uprightness and integrity, desiring to please the One who saved them. Yet that won't be easy. Satan is ready for battle at every turn, willing to hit us unfairly from behind if given the chance. Righteousness is the opposite of Satan's complete wickedness. Satan seeks to thwart righteous living.

- When the enemy, the accuser (Revelation 12:10), tries to convince us that we are not really saved, that we just keep on disappointing God, and that we're "poor excuses" for Christians, we can stand up to him because of the righteousness we have been promised through our faith in Jesus Christ. "This righteousness from God comes through faith in Jesus Christ to all who believe" (Romans 3:22, niv).[334]

### Illustration:

- I used to live my life as though I wasn't good enough to be called,

---

[333] Ingram, *The Invisible War*, 102-103.
[334] Barton and Comfort, *Ephesians*, 132.

"A Christian." I would engage in promiscuity, overindulge in alcohol, and rarely show up at church. But then, God made me realize that to Him, I am already a saint, now I needed to act like it. My righteousness or "right standing before the Father" is not because of anything I could ever achieve, but because Christ has already achieved it for me. I used to look at myself as a sinner trying to become a saint; God sees me as a saint who sins.

### Conclusion:

- Wear your breastplate of righteousness proudly. You have been bought at a price and Satan cannot take away the inheritance you've received through your genuine faith and love for Christ.
- Let's Pray

Week Five

"Peaceful Feet"

*Ephesians 6:15*

**Subject:** How can we maintain a solid foundation when fighting the enemy?

**Compliment:** By making sure our footing is rooted in the gospel message

**BI:** Only through the gospel of peace can we prevent falling into the enemy's hands.

### Introduction:

- Imagine putting on the belt of truth to guard against Satan's deceptions and the breastplate of righteousness to guard against his condemnation. Your vital organs are protected. But what good will that do if you can't keep your footing? You need a solid foundation that will keep you from falling.[335]

**Defensive Spiritual Armor**

• The soldier wore special sandals or military shoes that protected his feet without slowing him down. Roman soldiers had special shoes made of soft leather with studded soles. This allowed them to march farther and faster as well as giving them the facility of motion in battle—they could dig in and hold their ground when in hand-to-hand combat.

    A. Believers also need special "shoes"—*the readiness that comes from the gospel of peace.* The Word of God is the gospel, or Good News, that brings peace. In other words, believers are ready for battle because "the peace of God, which surpasses all understanding, will guard [their] hearts and minds through Christ Jesus" (Philippians 4:7 nkjv). They can stand firm, with peace, even in hand-to-hand combat, because they know that they are doing right and that they are on the winning side. Christians are in the battle both with the inner peace Christ has already given and the desire to produce that peace in the hearts of others. This can only happen as they share this "gospel of peace" with those who have not yet heard and accepted it.

    B. When the enemy, the deceiver (Revelation 12:9), offers false ways to peace or tries to get us to focus on our concerns and fears, we Christian soldiers can stand up to him. Jesus promised, "Peace I leave with you, my peace I give to you; not as the world gives do, I give to you. Let not your heart be troubled, neither let it be afraid" (John 14:27 nkjv).[336]

---

[335] Ingram, *The Invisible War*, 113.
[336] Barton and Comfort, *Ephesians*, 133.

**Illustration:**

- When I was around six years old, we used to ride our bikes in the neighborhood for fun. Now, it's like no kids want to get out of the house, but back in my day, there were no computers, so we actually played outside. One time, I was riding on the back of my friends' bike without my shoes. Unfortunately, my foot got caught in his spokes, and down we went. Instead of helping me up, he just dislodged my foot and left me in the middle of the street! He was scared, I'm sure. Fortunately, a neighbor heard me screaming and brought me into my parent's house. I had a cast and was fine after a few months. If I had shoes on, I probably wouldn't have broken my foot, and possibly, wouldn't have got it caught in the spokes because my shoe would have been too large to fit in there. I wasn't thinking defensively.

**Conclusion:**

- Much like my poor choice when preparing my body for battle, we must think ahead when we put on our spiritual armor. We need a solid foundation before we can ever have the victory. Are your foundational shoes of peace rooted in the Gospel?

- Let's Pray

Week Six

"The Shield of Faith"

*Ephesians 6:16*

**Subject:** How do we protect ourselves from Satan's arrows?

**Compliment:** With the shield of faith

**BI:** We extinguish Satan's flaming arrows with faith

**Introduction:**

- Faith is something that we hope for, but cannot see (Hebrews 11:1, emphasis mine). In this context, our confidence is in God, his promises, his power, and his program for our lives. Though rooted in the objective reality of the gospel and our new standing with God (justification) through Christ (saving faith), this faith refers to our "present faith in the Lord Jesus for victory over sin and the host of demonic forces."[337]

## Defensive Spiritual Armor

- *With all* the pieces of armor mentioned above, the soldier needed to also carry extra protection in the form of a *shield.* The image was taken from the Roman shield, a large oblong or oval piece, approximately four feet high by two feet wide, made of wood and leather, often with an iron frame. Sometimes the leather would be soaked in water to help extinguish *flaming arrows.* The ancient "flaming arrow" or "fire dart" was made of cane with a flammable head that was lighted and then shot so as to set fire to wooden shields, cloth tents, etc. For Christians, this shield is *faith*—complete reliance on God. Faith means total dependence on God and willingness to do his will. It is not something we put on for a show for others. It means believing in his promises even though we don't see those promises materializing yet. God gives faith to protect the believer (Ephesians 2.8). (see James 1:31 and Peter 1:7 for more on faith as the key to victory.)

  A. When the enemy, the ruler of this world (John 12:31), sends his flaming arrows of temptation, doubt, wrath, lust, despair, vengeance, problems, and trials into our lives, we can hold up our shields and *quench* them. We are assured that "whatever is born of God conquers the world. And this is the victory that conquers the world, our faith" (1 John 5:4 nrsv). We must take hold of God's full resources. Faith gives us the strength to stand against Satan with firm

---

[337] Ingram, *The Invisible War,* 123.

courage, even when he uses his most fearsome weapons.[338]

**Illustration:**

- Faith is so important. Often, I'll encounter a situation in which there is literally no way out. I've had times in my life where I've had run-ins with some sketchy people who wanted to do me harm, but I kept the faith and God got me through the situation. Faith also requires that we accept Jesus with our hearts and not just our minds.

**Conclusion:**

- Our shields of faith protect us when the enemy fires his arrows of temptation, lust, depression, and many other oppressive thoughts and desires. We must always have faith that God will be there for us and help us to get through any spiritual situation in which the enemy intends to do us harm.

- Let's Pray

Week Seven

"The Helmet of Salvation"

*Ephesians 6:17a*

**Subject:** How can we know that our salvation is secure

**Compliment:** by the hope that is given to all believers

**BI:** We are saved by grace alone through faith alone in Christ alone

---

[338] Barton and Comfort, *Ephesians*, 133–134.

**Introduction:**

- The last piece of armor a soldier would put on was his helmet. It was made of bronze and leather, and its importance was obvious: if you're hit on the head, you're out. So, immediately before going into battle, an attendant would bring a soldier his helmet and help him fasten it securely.[339]

**Defensive Spiritual Armor**

- First Thessalonians 5:8 calls believers to put on "the hope of salvation as a helmet." This "hope" is a certainty—believers have complete assurance that God will do all that he has promised. Their salvation, already accomplished, will be consummated when Christ comes to claim his own. Christians, with the assurance of salvation protecting their minds, can stand against Satan's attacks. As a blow to the head often means death, so a person without hope of salvation will be easily defeated by the enemy.

    A. When the enemy, the devil (1 Peter 5:8), seeks to devour and destroy God's people with empty or evil thoughts, trying to get us to doubt our salvation, we can trust in the protection of the helmet. Our salvation will be accomplished, for God has promised it. "Hope does not disappoint us" (Romans 5:5 niv) because "our salvation is nearer now than when we first believed" (Romans 13:11 niv).[340]

**Illustration:**

- I had coffee a few years ago with a friend of mine who was having some marital issues and wanted my counsel. I empathized with him, listened closely to his admonitions and concerns. After a short

---

[339] Ingram, *The Invisible War*, 148.
[340] Barton and Comfort, Ephesians, 134.

time, he said to me, "I don't even know if I'll end up in heaven." I told him that the fact that he is questioning that tells me where his heart is at. When we question if God is accepting of us, then we know that we have the hope of salvation in Christ Jesus. When we get complacent with our Christianity and take our salvation for granted, start to worry because the fruit of the Spirit may not be quite ripe yet.

### Conclusion:

- Our salvation is secure in Christ Jesus if we have placed our faith and trust in Him. The enemy cannot take that away from us, no matter what he tells you. Often, I'll rebuke the devil as soon as I hear that voice in my head that begins to question if Christ was truly God, or if I'm good enough to be a pastor, etc.

- Let's Pray

*Week Eight*

"The Sword of the Spirit"

*Ephesians 6:17b*

**Subject:** How can we attack Satan?

**Compliment:** with the sword of the Spirit

**BI:** The Sword of the Spirit is God's Word; we must use it wisely against the enemy

### Introduction:

- For the past seven weeks, we've looked at the defensive spiritual armor that Christians already possess to help them defeat the day to day battles of the enemy. Christ, of course, has already defeated the eternal consequences of the enemy, which is death itself. Yet, day to day battles still occur and we must defend ourselves against them. This week, we'll look at the only offensive weapon that's listed in Ephesians chapter six.

**The Offensive Spiritual Weapon used to Attack the Enemy**

- **The sword of the Spirit, which is the word of God.** Finally, the soldier takes *the sword of the Spirit*—the only offensive weapon mentioned. This refers to the short sword used in close combat. The sharp, short sword was one of Rome's great military innovations. The Roman army was called the "short swords" because of its use of the short swords in winning battles. The sword's double edges made it ideal for the "cut and thrust" strategy. The relative pronoun translated *which* could refer to "the Spirit" or to the whole phrase, "sword of the Spirit." The Word of God is the Spirit's sword (see Isaiah 11:4–5; 2 Thessalonians 2:8; Hebrews 4:12).

- The Spirit makes the Word of God effective as we speak it and receive it. The Spirit gives the Word its penetrating power and sharp edge. Jesus' use of God's Word in his temptation prompts our use of it against Satan (Matthew 4:4, 7, 10). With the Holy Spirit within, believers have the constant reminder of God's Word to use against Satan's temptations.[341]

**Illustration:**

- It's so important to read our Bibles daily! When we go out into the world, we get dirtied up by the sin around us. What better way to wash ourselves off than with the Word of God? We are so much more prepared to defeat the enemy when we utilize God's Word properly against him. Jesus was tempted in the wilderness for forty days and forty nights. When Satan incorrectly applied God's words, Jesus corrected him and prevailed against Satan's temptations. We can do the same. The

---

[341] Barton and Comfort, Ephesians, 134.

Lord Jesus has provided all the weapons we need. Christ has provided all of our victories. He used the same tools that He now provides for us in winning the battle.[342]

## Conclusion:

- The Sword of the Spirit is literally God's Word. It's both the physical words written in the Bible and His Word, also known as Jesus Christ. Use them both to attack the enemy before he attacks you. Satan cannot stand to hear the truth, so what better way to go on the offensive against him.

- Let's Pray

*Week Nine*

"Pray at All Times"

*Ephesians 6:18*

**Subject:** How should we pray against the Evil One?

**Compliment:** In and with the Holy Spirit

**BI:** Believers must pray in the Spirit at all times against the attacks of the Devil.

### Introduction:

a. Prayer is the chief means by which we employ and appropriate the victory that is ours over all principalities and powers. The mighty resources in prayer remain yet to be tapped in most believers' lives.[343]

---

[342] Bubeck, *The Adversary*, 165-166.
[343] Ibid., 126.

b.  Jesus Christ, Himself prayed all night before choosing His disciples (Lk. 6:12).

## The Power of Prayer

- This verse, although not naming another "weapon" in the believers' armor, does continue the thought of 6:17. As we take the sword of the Spirit, God's Word, we must also *pray in the Spirit on all occasions*. Praying in the Spirit means that the Spirit helps us when we pray (Romans 8:26); the Spirit prays on our behalf (Romans 8:27); the Spirit makes God accessible (Ephesians 2:18); the Spirit gives us confidence when we pray (Romans 8:15–16; Galatians 4:6). He inspires and guides us when we pray. He helps us communicate with God and also brings God's response to us.

- Paul was not calling prayer a weapon; instead, he was giving the how-tos for taking up the armor described in the previous verses. We must not underestimate Satan's forces. He will strike in different ways at different people; thus, we need to pray "all kinds" of prayers, allowing for all kinds of requests. Satan will attack at various times, but he will always be attacking someone. Believers need to be praying *always*. Satan will attack when we least expect it, so we need to be *alert* to prayer needs when they arise. Satan will rarely let up if he thinks he can win the battle, so believers must *keep on* praying, no matter how long it takes. No believer is exempt from being Satan's target—Satan demands battle against his enemies (believers).[344]

## Illustration:

- Not long ago, I took an excellent prayer class at MU. We not only prayed daily, but we prayed specifically for various categories like praise, listening for God to speak, worship, confession, thanksgiv-

---

[344] Barton and Comfort, Ephesians, 136.

ing, intercession, etc. God spoke to me quite a bit during those prayer times. He will surely speak to you as well.

### Conclusion:

- Praying in the Spirit at all times can also be phrased, "pray *with* the Spirit at all times."[345] So, this verse does not mean we must speak in tongues, but rather, that we should utilize the power of the Holy Spirit during our prayer time. Because Satan does not give up, we must not give up praying to God to deliver us from the Evil One.

- Let's Pray

*Week Ten*

"Spiritual Oppression"

*2 Timothy 1:7*

**Subject:** Can a Christian be possessed by the Devil?

**Compliment:** no, but they can face demonic oppression

**BI:** A believer may be afflicted or even controlled in certain areas of his being, but he can never be owned or totally controlled as an unbeliever.

### Introduction:

- Some believers are afraid of being possessed by the devil. Yet,

---

[345] en pneumati (a atoV) **"In the Spirit"** - in/by/with spirit. The preposition en is local, expressing space/sphere; the sphere within which the prayers operate, but possibly instrumental, "by". Possibly "spiritual prayer", Phillips, but usually taken to mean "the Holy Spirit", the one who guides and inspires believers through the word of God. See "An Exegetical Commentary on the Greek New Testament," Pumpkin Cottage Ministry Resources, accessed March 4, 2020, http://www.lectionarystudies.com/studyn/sunday21bacn.html.

fear comes from a different spirit. Satan and his demons are quick to author fear. The apostle Peter calls us to be sober and vigilant because our adversary prowls around like a roaring lion looking for those to devour (1 Pet. 5:8-9, emphasis mine).[346]

**Four Gifts of the Spirit:**

- Timothy experienced constant opposition to his message and himself as a leader. His youth (see 1 Timothy 4:12), his association with Paul, and his leadership had come under fire from believers and nonbelievers alike. Perhaps Timothy felt intimidated, angered, even helpless in face of the opposition from the false teachers. Whatever the degree of his difficulties, Paul urged Timothy to boldness by reminding him of his call, his gift, and God's provision (see 1:6). God does *not* give *a spirit of fear,* that is, timidity or cowardice; rather God provides:

- *Power*—We do not need to have naturally powerful personalities. God gives strength of character and confidence that wins us respect when we face opposition as we speak, preach, and live the truth. God supernaturally replaces any timidity on the servant's part with boldness. The powerful minister doesn't hoard his power or lord it over others; he empowers those in his congregation.

- *Love*—Accompanying the power to speak the truth must be love for the listeners, believers, and nonbelievers alike. Love separates Christians from the heathen world around them. Jesus promised, "By this, all will know that you are My disciples if you have love for one another" (John 13:35 nkjv). Indeed, love separated the minister of Christ from the false teachers. Such love is difficult to dismiss.

- *Self-discipline*—This can also be translated as "self-control" or "sound mind." In order to lead others, the true minister must have control over himself. To put it another way, a good leader must

---

[346] Bubeck, *The Adversary*, 94.

have a cool head. Self-discipline and self-control sound like *self-effort*. But Paul explained them as divinely bestowed on his servants, resulting in the soundness of mind. Such control, such "soundness" is difficult to disclaim.[347]

**Illustration:**

- Traveling around town late at night, it's easy to see people who are facing demonic oppression and even possession. Some diagnose them medically or psychologically, but I like to also inquire about their spiritual lives and if they have been involved in occult practices that may have let something in. Remember to test the spirits to be sure they are godly ones.

**Conclusion:**

- I've only ever heard of people being oppressed, but never actually witnessed anyone who claims they are oppressed or possessed. The difference between oppression and possession is who is controlling your soul. A Christian's soul is possessed only by the Holy Spirit; therefore, he cannot be possessed by the devil.
- Let's Pray

---

[347] Barton, Veerman, and Wilson, 1 Timothy, 2 Timothy, Titus, 161–163.

# ABOUT AUTHOR

CRAIG M PRATHER is an adjunct professor of Bible and Theology at Multnomah University-Nevada. Professor Prather is a local pastor and has an M.Div. with a concentration in Spiritual Formation from Multnomah University. Craig currently serves at 1$^{st}$ Church of God in Reno and is the author of, *Moved by the Spirit: A Daily Devotional & Living Doxology.* Craig lives in Reno, Nevada with his wife and three children.

# ABOUT
# KHARIS PUBLISHING

**KHARIS PUBLISHING** is an independent, traditional publishing house with a core mission to publish impactful books, and channel proceeds into establishing mini-libraries or resource centers for orphanages in developing countries, so these kids will learn to read, dream, and grow. Every time you purchase a book from Kharis Publishing or partner as an author, you are helping give these kids an amazing opportunity to read, dream, and grow. Kharis Publishing is an imprint of Kharis Media LLC. Learn more at **https://www.kharispublishing.com**.

www.ingramcontent.com/pod-product-compliance
Lightning Source LLC
Chambersburg PA
CBHW062101080426
42734CB00012B/2714